Manage Your Anger

Sandi Mann

Hodder Education

338 Euston Road, London NW1 3BH.

Hodder Education is an Hachette UK company

First published in UK 2012 by Hodder Education

First published in US 2012 by The McGraw-Hill Companies, Inc.

This edition published 2012

British Library Cataloguing in Publication Data: a catalogue record for this title is available from the British Library.

Library of Congress Catalog Card Number: on file.

10 9 8 7 6 5 4 3 2

www.hoddereducation.co.uk

Cover image © Michael Flippo – Fotolia

Typeset by Cenveo Publisher Services.

Printed in Great Britain by CPI Group (UK) Ltd, Croydon, CR0 4YY.

Also available in ebook

Dr Sandi Mann is a senior psychology lecturer at the University of Central Lancashire and Director of the MindTraining Clinic. She is a specialist in workplace emotions, including anger, and has previously authored *Anger Management in a Week* (Hodder, 2004) as well as academic journals and practitioner articles in the field. She also delivers training on anger management to organizations and individuals both through her university and her clinic.

Contents

Introduction

Everyone knows what it is to be angry, but for some people anger can be a significant problem. Anger, if felt too intensely or too often, or if expressed inappropriately, can be a cause for concern. This book attempts to address these problems by guiding you through the tools of anger management, using a series of interactive exercises.

When trying to manage your anger, it is important to remember that anger, like all emotions, has a useful function, and this book is not about trying to encourage you not to feel anger, or even not to show it. Anger, when felt and expressed appropriately, is an important part of anger management, and this book takes you through the process of achieving this. You will learn techniques that will enable you to become less stressed and less 'anger-prone'; by using humour, cognitive techniques and channelling you can make anger work for you, not against you.

Of course, some situations can make even the calmest of individuals react with anger. This book aims to help you cope with those times when the red mist is most likely to descend – such as when encountering abusive customers, unhelpful shop assistants, delayed planes or other motorists. Sometimes, however, it is not our own anger that is the issue, but the anger of other people, and conflict management has a vital role to play when dealing with other people's rage – even when those other people are our own children.

This book is designed to be worked through from cover to cover but can also be used to dip into on a chapter-by-chapter basis as required. However you use it, you will learn how to control anger, not let it control you.

1

The nature of anger

How do you feel?
Answer yes or no to the following questions.

- *Do you feel that you understand what anger is?*
- *Do you feel that you get angry too often?*
- *Do you feel that you express your anger inappropriately?*
- *Do you feel that there is any point in getting angry?*
- *Do you know what sorts of incidents cause you to get angry?*

The aim of these questions is to stimulate some thought about the nature of anger; this chapter aims to answer these questions.

What exactly is anger?

> *'Anybody can become angry – that is easy, but to be angry with the right person and to the right degree and at the right time and for the right purpose, and in the right way – that is not within everybody's power and is not easy.'*
>
> Aristotle

Most of us are familiar with anger – whether our own or that of other people. It is a rare person who does not know what it is to feel angry. In fact, according to a recent poll by the Mental Health Foundation (in their report *Boiling Point: Problem anger and what we can do about it*, 2008), more than a quarter of people worry about just how angry they sometimes feel. Various terms are used to describe feeling angry such as *furious, in a rage, flipping out, in a temper, losing my temper, annoyed, freaking out, going crazy, mad, at the end of my tether/rope, flying off the handle, cheesed off, enraged, fuming* and many others less repeatable here!

There might be many ways to describe anger but they all reflect the same thing – an emotion. Like most human emotions, anger is actually a healthy part of our emotional repertoire; it is our body and brain's way of signalling that all is not right in our world and that action is needed to rectify a wrong. Most emotions have an evolutionary purpose; that is, they exist to aid our survival. Our cave-dwelling ancestors in the past would have experienced anger when a rival stole their food or prized possessions; this strong emotion would have stimulated them into action to fight for their rights. Without anger, our ancestors would have lazily allowed all their food to be stolen from under their noses and would not have survived long.

> **Point to remember**
>
> Anger has a valuable adaptive purpose and can play an important role in our lives.

Today, anger can be used for the same purpose – perhaps not to stop our dinner being stolen, but to galvanize us into action when we feel our rights are being threatened (more on this later in this chapter). The issue here is that many of us experience too much anger for too much of the time; this is when anger becomes a problem. Anger researchers such as Dahlen and Deffenbacher (2001) believe that the most comprehensive explanation of anger is one that includes four separate elements and that we only experience real anger when all four facets are present. These are:

1 the *feeling* of being angry
This feeling can range in intensity from mild annoyance to over-powering rage or fury.

2 some sort of *bodily change*, called physiological arousal
This is often caused by the release of adrenalin, which causes a range of reactions in our body (such as increased heart rate and blood pressure); more on this in chapter 2.

3 a *mental or cognitive awareness* that an event has occurred that threatens us in some way
Without being able to interpret an event in this way, we would not feel anger (which is why different people can witness the same event but only some would be angered by it).

4 an effect on our *behaviour*

To really feel anger, we need to express it in some way – for example by hitting someone or shouting (aggressive and inappropriate expression of anger) or writing a letter of complaint (a more appropriate expression of anger); more on these in chapters 3 and 4.

Myth buster
Some people believe that 'anger is all in the mind'. This is not true; the mind plays only one part in the anger process. It is true that, to feel anger, we must have some sort of mind process going on, but real anger is felt throughout the body – sometimes before our minds have even labelled what we are experiencing as 'anger'.

How anger differs from frustration, aggression and rage

Anger is often confused with rage, frustration and aggression. It is useful to separate these terms to help understand them and their relationship to anger.

▶ **Frustration** or irritability is often a precursor to anger; it is the feeling we experience when we don't get what we want, when obstacles are put in our way or when someone else interferes (deliberately or not) with our attempts at achieving our goals.

▶ **Aggression,** on the other hand, is the action that can result from being very angry. It is usually intended to cause physical or emotional harm to others, perhaps with verbal insults, threats, sarcasm or raised voices. When aggression becomes so extreme that we lose self-control, it is said that we are in a **rage**; such a person is typically very loud (perhaps shouting), may be red in the face, threatening and perhaps even physically abusive.

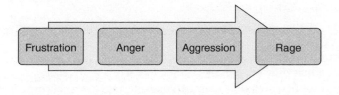

Frustration → Anger → Aggression → Rage

Max arrives at work late after a traffic accident delays his commute. He is frustrated because he just wants to get on with his day but can't. To add to his frustration, his lateness means that there are no spaces left in his usual car park so he has to drive around for 20 minutes. His sense of frustration at not being able to start work is building even before he sets foot in his office.

Once at his desk – in an open-plan office – Max is constantly interrupted by phone calls, emails and colleagues. He has two reports to complete and did expect to have enough time to do them, but the constant interruptions delay him considerably. His irritability is growing. Then his wife rings to say that their child is ill and Max will have to go and fetch him from school because she is in clinic all day. At this, Max's frustration boils over into anger and he snarls and swears at his wife, telling her that she will have to make the arrangements for their child herself.

He has only just put the phone down when an email arrives from his boss asking where Max's report is. Although it isn't due in till the end of the day, his boss wants to check it first, so needs it earlier. Trying to suppress his anger, Max works on it quickly, ignoring phone calls, emails and even texts from his wife. By 2 p.m., his hunger is too distracting and he is forced to abandon his work for a sprint to the coffee shop around the corner. The long queue there does nothing to dampen his feelings of frustration, irritability and suppressed anger. Then, someone cuts in front of him, claiming that they have been in front all along. That does it: Max explodes with rage, shouting and swearing at the customer and jabbing his finger aggressively towards him. He is asked to leave the shop, but he just gets angrier. The customer finally lets him go in front, he gets his sandwich and goes back to work – and now he can't help wondering what on earth got into him to make him behave so badly.

Identifying anger

Emotions are often difficult to distinguish from each other, especially if they are closely related, like stress and anger. An important first step in learning to manage anger is to become better at identifying our emotions. This exercise will help you become more in tune with your experience of anger.

Step 1: Recall an episode that has made you feel very angry recently. Write down what happened.

Step 2: How did the incident make you feel? Examine your emotions carefully. What words would you use to describe how you felt? Anger may only be part of what you felt. Did you feel sad? Disappointed? Worried? Did you feel you had been treated unfairly?

Step 3: Did you feel any changes within your body? For example, did you feel hot? Did you feel that your blood pressure was rising? Did your muscles feel tense?

Step 4: What action did you take? Perhaps you wanted to take a certain action (maybe even wanting to hit someone) but didn't?

Step 5: Could this incident have happened to someone else – without making them feel as angry? What sort of person would not have got angry? How would they have been different from you?

Outcomes of this exercise

This exercise will help you become more in tune with the emotions that surround an angry episode. It is the first stage to better management of your anger.

▶ **Step 1** starts by encouraging you to recall an angry episode; this can be quite hard because incidents that made us angry in the past may no longer stir the same intensity of feeling now. This in itself is an important discovery from this exercise.
▶ **Step 2** is about helping you to unscramble the range of emotions that you might previously have labelled as 'anger'. This will enable you to become more discerning about labelling an emotion as anger.
▶ **Step 3** helps you to understand how anger affects your body, which will help you appreciate why it is so important to manage your anger (for more on this see chapter 2). Recognizing the changes in your body that anger causes is also part of learning about the feedback loop that can teach you when your anger is becoming a problem (see chapter 3).

▶ **Step 4** helps you to start looking at whether the outcomes of your anger are healthy or not in terms of the actions you take; this is the first step to turning these consequences into more positive ones (see chapter 4).

▶ Finally, **Step 5** starts you thinking about whether you have an 'angry personality'; this is discussed more in chapter 3.

Quick fix
Understanding your anger and the emotions associated with it is the first step to managing it.

The purpose and function of anger

Myth buster
It is generally assumed by most people that anger is bad. People who are slow to anger, or who are calm under pressure and never lose their cool, are seen as models to aspire to. This is wrong. Anger *per se* is not bad; it is when and how we express it that can cause the problems. It can be just as 'bad' not to get angry; people who never get angry may not have a strong enough self-esteem to recognize their rights. They may also put up with abuse or injustice because they don't get angry enough to do anything about it.

It is now worth taking a step back and considering the purpose of anger. As mentioned earlier, anger is an emotion and, like all emotions, evolved in humans for a reason. A range of functions is proposed for the emotion of anger and these functions are worth looking at in detail because anger gets such a bad press. Anger is seen as the 'baddie' of emotions. It is portrayed as something to be 'managed', 'controlled' and 'beaten'. Expressing anger is seen as bad while suppressing it is viewed as harmful.

All this is true (as will be outlined in the next chapter) but it is worth pointing out, at this early stage in your anger management journey, that anger is not necessarily the bad guy that it is made out to be. Anger is only 'bad' when:

▶ it is experienced too much (i.e. if we get angry too often)
▶ it is experienced with too much intensity (i.e. we feel excessively angry)
▶ it is expressed inappropriately (e.g. by being aggressive).

Anger is not in itself a problem; it is only a problem if we have too much of it or express it in an inappropriate way.

Even in these circumstances, the aim of anger management programmes and books such as this should never be to eliminate anger but to learn to use it for the purpose and function for which it was intended. These functions include the following.

1 To get what we want or need

Researchers at the Center for Evolutionary Psychology in America (2009) consider anger to be a behaviour-regulating programme that evolved over time. They proposed that the reason for the evolution of this emotion through natural selection was to help an individual bargain better for what they want or need to survive.

This works because expressed anger can encourage the target of that anger to offer something that might reduce the likelihood of them suffering in any way from the angry outburst (e.g. by being attacked). In other words, Tom wants something from Fred. Fred says no. Tom gets angry. Fred is afraid and says yes. Mission accomplished.

This use of anger to achieve this function might well be attempted in modern times (see the following case study) but is unlikely to work quite so well in most societies around the world today. In fact, many organizations these days adopt a 'zero-tolerance' policy towards this kind of attempt to use anger as a bargaining tool. (See the three examples in the second case study below.)

Assaults on job centre staff

According to a report in *The Independent* newspaper (21 December 2009), more than 1,000 staff at Jobcentre Plus offices around the country are being abused, threatened or assaulted every month. It seems that recession-hit and cash-strapped jobseekers are increasingly likely to take out their frustrations on the job centre staff who are trying to help them – something that the then Shadow Work and Pensions Secretary Theresa May denounced as 'shocking'. In response to this increased tendency to abuse staff, Work and Pensions minister Jonathan Shaw has introduced a 'zero tolerance' approach, whereby staff are encouraged to report all incidents of unacceptable behaviour, however minor they may seem.

Abuse of staff: zero tolerance policies

Example a

'We will not tolerate any violence or abuse towards any of the surgery staff at any time. Anybody exhibiting inappropriate behaviour may be removed from the Practice List. More serious episodes will be reported to the police.'

Sign in GP Practice, Wales

Example b

'In order to ensure that all patients attending this department receive the treatment they need, it is essential that our staff are able to work without fear of attack, abuse or harassment. This Trust views its staff as its most valuable asset and therefore any abuse to those staff is totally unacceptable. Staff are encouraged to report all incidents of harassment and violence.'

North Middlesex University Hospital NHS Trust

Example c

'No abuse of staff or any other person on the practice premises is acceptable whether verbal or physical. The practice defines aggressive behaviour to be any personal, abusive and aggressive comments, bad language, physical contact and aggressive gestures.'

Medical Centre, Glasgow

In order, then, to make use of this function of anger, it is imperative that anger is expressed in an appropriate way that is neither aggressive nor abusive. Techniques to do this will be outlined in chapter 4.

Anger management is not about getting rid of anger – it is about learning to use it better.

2 To prepare us for action

Anger, like stress, sends signals to all parts of our body to help us fight or flee. It energizes us to prepare us for action. We will discuss in more detail how it does this in chapter 2, but for now it is useful to understand this valuable function that anger has. Without anger, we would not be mentally and physically able to take the action required to right a wrong (or perceived wrong) against us.

The drawback of this function of anger, in evolutionary terms, is that the action that anger prepares us for is physical. Today, engaging in violence is not an appropriate response to being wronged, and so we must learn to override this natural instinct in order to channel this readiness more appropriately.

3 To tell us when our rights have been violated

Anger tells us when something has happened that is a violation or abuse; it helps protect us from unjust or threatening action and also from any future abuse from that abuser. Thus, we can only get angry when we have some sense of entitlement or some acceptance of our rights. When these rights are violated, it is appropriate for us to get angry. Part of learning to manage our anger is about understanding what our rights are and when they are being violated.

Understanding and acknowledging the 'right to be angry' is an important step in anger management. Sometimes people can be over-sensitive to their rights (they have a sense of over-entitlement and think they have more rights than they do – which leads them to become angry too often) and sometimes they can be under-sensitive (believing that they have few rights and thus not getting angry enough).

This is dealt with in more detail in chapter 4.

4 To change things

Anger is a very motivating emotion: it can stimulate us to make changes to our circumstances in order to reduce the causes of our anger. For example, if elements of our job anger us, we might be able to make changes to our working pattern (or even look for a new job); if contact with a certain organization is what gets us going, we might switch our allegiance to a competitor. Anger can also motivate us to try to persuade other people to change.

Anger over changes to pension leads to one-day strike

According to a report in *Wigan Today* (24 March 2011), teachers were so angry about planned changes to their pension scheme that they staged a one-day strike across the region. The teachers were members of the University and College Union (UCU) and the action was part of the first UK-wide strike in universities for five years.

5 To express tension and to communicate negative feelings

Sometimes our feelings stay bottled up until we get angry. The constructive expression of anger can be a way to resolve conflict, as will be seen in chapter 7. By expressing anger appropriately, we can let other people know that we are unhappy.

The problem with using anger for this function is getting the balance right between letting others know that we are angry and not getting too angry. Many people are too understated in this and may send unclear messages out so that their anger is pretty much ignored. Sometimes you can get your message across only by expressing your anger strongly, but there is a danger that expressing it too strongly can come across as aggressive.

Sarvinder's story

Sarvinder lives near a school on a quiet road in the suburbs. She is concerned, however, at the speed at which cars zoom down this road, especially given that there are schoolchildren about. Her own children walk to school and she worries about their safety.

One icy day in winter, a car going too fast skidded and smashed into a wall, narrowly missing Sarvinder's six-year-old son. Her son avoided injury only because she was able to pull him out of the way.

Sarvinder decides that enough is enough and that she is going to try to get the council to make the road safer.

She rings her local council but her concerns are dismissed. She is told, quite abruptly she thinks, that no traffic-calming measures can be taken 'until some children are actually hit by cars'. They refuse even to come down and take any measures or to look at the problem. Because no child has been injured – yet – no action will be taken. This makes Sarvinder angry. She feels that it is unjust and unethical that a child has to be injured or preferably killed before they will even monitor the traffic problem.

She is so angry that she starts telling other parents at the school about the attitude of the council. While this makes her feel better initially, she is still angry that nothing can be done. She decides to take action herself and get the council to change its mind – and at least come and monitor the amount of traffic and their speeds. She sets up a FaceBook page and Twitter account to encourage people to support her action. Hundreds do and she begins petitions, calls meetings and gets the local press on board.

Her actions work and the council finally agrees to monitor the traffic on her road. It takes two years but traffic-calming humps are eventually installed to slow cars down – before a child is injured or killed.

Point to remember

Sometimes we need to feel angry to create change.

WHAT DO YOU WANT YOUR ANGER TO ACHIEVE?

The next time you find yourself getting angry, stop and think about the function you want your anger to achieve. Look at the five functions below and try to decide on the one that would best fit your current emotional state. Then ask yourself the following questions.

The purpose of your anger	Questions to ask
1 To get something I want or need	• What do I want? • How can I realistically get this? • Can I suggest a compromise?
2 To prepare me for action	• What action can I take here? • What action is appropriate? • What action is inappropriate?
3 To alert me that my rights have been violated	• What rights have been violated? • Am I sure I have those rights? • Am I targeting my anger appropriately (i.e. at the violator of my rights)?
4 To effect some change	• What change do I want to make? • How do I want others to change? • How can I realistically achieve this change?
5 To communicate my dissatisfaction	• Has this been achieved? • Who do I want to hear my message? • What is the best way to communicate my anger (spoken, email, letter, etc.)?

Quick fix

Working out what you want to achieve by your anger can help you use anger appropriately.

The causes of anger

Many things can make us angry. From road rage to phone rage, the causes of anger today seem limitless. Sometimes other people make us angry; sometimes we are angry with ourselves or even with inanimate objects (computers are a good example – see chapter 10).

All the things that make us angry, however, can be categorized within a relatively small number of themes. These themes can help us understand the causes of our anger more clearly. By looking at the categories into which our sources of anger commonly fall, we are more able to select appropriate ways of dealing with these causes, especially if we can identify common themes.

What makes you angry?

Do the following exercise to begin examining the main sources of anger in your life.

Which of the following situations would be most likely to make you angry? Select no more than ten of the following situations that you think would make you angriest.

1 Someone else stealing your ideas at work   C
2 Phone calls interrupting you   A
3 Computer crashing while you are doing something important   A
4 Kids interrupting you while you are trying to get something done   A
5 Being unable to find a parking space   D
6 Being told what to do without being consulted   G
7 Being let down by somebody F
8 People gossiping about you B
9 Getting a parking ticket when you were two minutes late back   C
10 Being stuck in traffic   A
11 New systems (involving new training) being implemented at work when you don't know what was wrong with the old ones   G
12 The photocopier at work breaking down yet again   H
13 Your local supermarket charging you the wrong amount at the checkout yet again   H
14 Queues   A
15 Someone else blaming you for something you didn't do   C
16 Someone else getting angry with you   B
17 Your friend getting the part in the play you wanted   C
18 When things don't go according to plan   D
19 Your colleague taking an unwarranted 'sickie' from work   E
20 An able-bodied person using a disabled parking space   E
21 Someone else refusing to take or return your calls   B
22 Poor customer service   D
23 Other people not doing what you tell them to do   F
24 Other people making mistakes   D

(contd)

25 Someone suing an organization for an injury that was far more minor than they claim   E

26 Someone lying to you   B

27 Another person grabbing the last sale bargain before you   C

28 Someone swearing at you or being rude to you   B

29 Your neighbour claiming benefits they are not entitled to   E

30 Your partner saying yes to your children after you said no   F

31 Your partner continually leaving wet towels on the floor   H

32 Your friend being repeatedly late when you arrange to meet for coffee   H

33 Travel delays without explanation   G

34 No one leaving you milk in the fridge   D

35 Your children leaving their rooms a mess   H

36 Someone you know buying clothes for a party, wearing them, then taking them back for a refund   E

37 Feeling that you have to do everything in the house without support from anyone else   F

38 When you tell a customer they can't have a refund but your boss overrides you   F

39 Your teenage son/daughter truanting from school but refusing to tell you why   G

40 Finding out that a meeting at work was arranged without you   G

How to score

Each of these causes of anger falls into one of four themes. Count up the As, Bs, Cs and Ds, etc., to see which theme is most likely to cause you anger.

A   Frustrations/irritations: things that block us from doing what we want or that thwart our goals

B   Abuse: when other people treat us badly or disrespect us

C   Injustice: when we believe we have been treated unfairly

D   Unmet expectations: when we expect something to happen and are disappointed when it does not

E Unethical behaviour: when another person behaves in an immoral way, perhaps taking advantage of someone or maybe acquiring something through dubious means

F Lack of support: feeling that other people are not supporting you or backing you up

G Lack of communication: when we are not kept informed about what is going on, kept out of the loop or otherwise not given a chance to discuss important issues

H Ongoing issues: when the same issue keeps recurring

NB: Some of the items could fall into more than one category depending on how you interpret the event. For example, 'not being able to find a parking space' has been put into category D here (unmet expectations) under the assumption that your anger is felt because you expected to find a space but were unable to. However, you might feel angry not because of unmet expectations but because the lack of parking causes a delay and thwarts your attempt to do something – which would be category A. Alternatively, you might react to the lack of a parking space by taking it personally, believing it 'so unfair'; you would then put this into category C.

This illustrates just how important individual interpretation is but, for the purposes of this exercise, the above categorizations will suffice; later on you will have the opportunity to personalize your own anger causes in a more in-depth exercise.

What your results mean

Count the As, Bs, Cs and so on and use the following list for an indication of what your scores mean; if no one category emerged as the most common for you, then read the sections for the top two or three themes you selected.

Mainly As: If frustrations and irritations are the main sources of your anger then stress could be an issue that is underlying your anger levels. When we are stressed, we are more affected by minor irritations and interruptions; this is why these things are often less likely to bother us on holiday when we are more relaxed. This will be dealt with in more detail in chapter 3.

Mainly Bs: When other people are disrespectful to us, it is natural to feel angry. However, while we can't always control how other people treat us, we can learn to control how we react. Techniques for managing anger elicited from these sources will be dealt with in chapter 7.

Mainly Cs: Some people have stronger anticipation of 'fairness' in life than others. Such people might find that they score mostly C in this quiz, because they feel more threatened when things that they perceive as 'unfair' happen to them. Some of this is tied up in the concept of an 'angry personality'; this will be examined in more detail in chapter 3.

Mainly Ds: It is natural to feel disappointed when our expectations in life are not met, but not everyone feels especially angry about this. If these are sources of anger for you, tackling them might involve altering your expectations rather than the way you react to them. There is more on this in chapter 3.

Mainly Es: If you get particularly angry at other people's lack of moral behaviour, then it is likely that you have high moral and ethical standards. This should be a good thing, but not if it is causing you to be angry too much! One way to manage this would be to learn to 'channel' that anger in appropriate ways; this will be examined in chapter 6.

Mainly Fs: If lack of support is a significant cause of your anger, you might need to look at the relationships in your life. If you feel you lack support from colleagues or family, or both, and you might need to tackle these anger sources head on; there is more on how to do this in chapter 7.

Mainly Gs: If information is being withheld from us, for example at work or by airlines and other service providers, we need to express our anger about this in appropriate ways. Losing our temper is never likely to achieve much to improve communication, so if this area is a source of anger for you, chapters 4 and 10 will be particularly useful.

Mainly Hs: For many people, all the previous categories can overlap with 'H' in that anything can become a bigger source of anger if it is done repeatedly. It is frustrating to feel that the same anger-inducing things keep happening over and over; whether they be ongoing technical problems, colleagues who keep doing annoying things or family members who just won't listen to your complaints. Learning to express your anger appropriately is vital here (see chapter 4), as is conflict resolution (see chapter 7, which looks at the reasons people may be unresponsive to repeated pleas).

If it is too hard to select only ten, and if the entire list covers significant sources of anger for you – and that is likely to be most readers – then you definitely need this book!

••
Quick fix
Working out the typical incidents that tend to make you angry is useful in helping you tackle anger sources.
••

Keeping a thematic anger source diary

The above exercise served as a useful introduction to the range of themes that sources of anger can fall into and how knowing which theme(s) are most relevant to you can help with tackling your anger. However, this exercise is necessarily limited in the items listed; now is the time to extend your learning from that exercise and develop a more personalized thematic anger source diary for yourself.

To do this, you will need to record your anger episodes over the next few weeks. Use a table like the one below to chart the sources of your anger episodes according to the themes outlined above. Make your own table with the headings shown and score your level of anger from 0 (not angry at all) to 100 (the most angry you have ever been), so as to be able to distinguish between mild annoyance (that might not need tackling) and major rage (that does). Remember that your anger source may well fall into more than one theme.

Example of thematic anger source diary

Episode that caused me to get angry	How angry did I get? 0 (not angry) – 100 (the most angry I could be)	Theme(s) that my anger source best falls into
I came home from a long day at work to find the breakfast things still on the table, no sign of any supper, the house a mess and the kids watching TV with their father.	60	C, D, F
I was desperately trying to finish off an important piece of work but everything went wrong: first the computer kept crashing, then my boss demanded an urgent response to something.	55	A
I booked seats for a theatre show well in advance, thinking they would be great seats; when I got there I saw that the view was restricted.	70	D, C

Use your completed diary to start identifying the most common or ongoing themes that your own anger episodes fall into. This will help you identify the best techniques for managing your anger according to the framework described above. It will be helpful to refer to your completed diary later in this book.

MOVING ON

This chapter has started you on your journey towards anger management by helping you understand both the point of getting angry and the reasons why you tend to get angry. Being aware of the functions of anger is vital because it demonstrates how anger can be good; the next chapter examines all the ways anger can be bad, so the two chapters together offer a healthy balance. Using an anger diary will help you identify the common themes that underlie your anger, and you can continue using the diary as you work your way through the rest of the book and focus on other aspects of the anger cycle.

Key points

1 Anger is not all in the mind; it affects the whole body.

2 Anger has many important functions and should not be regarded as 'bad'.

3 Being angry can motivate us to make changes or to encourage others to make changes.

4 Understanding the common things that typically cause our anger is an important first step to managing anger.

5 The ultimate aim should not be to eliminate anger but to manage it.

2

The consequences of anger

How do you feel?
Answer 'true' or 'false' to the following statements.

- *When I am angry I notice how it affects my body.* T/F
- *After I have been angry I sometimes feel depressed or resentful.* T/F
- *I tend to suppress my anger rather than let it all out.* T/F
- *When I am angry I sometimes take it out on other people.* T/F
- *Sometimes I get so angry that I just don't want to talk about it.* T/F

Both true and false responses can indicate that your anger has potentially serious consequences for you. Being unable to express our anger appropriately can adversely affect our physical and mental health and produce other destructive outcomes – for us and for others – as will be outlined in this chapter.

How anger affects our body

> *'How much more grievous are the consequences of anger than the causes of it.'*
>
> Marcus Aurelius

Most people think that anger is invariably 'bad' for us, without knowing why. Of course, by now we know that anger isn't necessarily bad and can be good for us too. Just to remind ourselves, anger is 'bad' when:

▶ it is experienced too much (i.e. if we get angry too often)
▶ it is experienced with too much intensity (i.e. we feel excessively angry)
▶ it is expressed inappropriately (e.g. by being aggressive).

Anger is bad for us if we experience it too often or too intensely and/or we express it inappropriately.

Assuming that one or more of the above conditions is in place, what exactly does anger do to us? Here, we will examine the physical effects of anger on our body. The next section looks at the effects that anger can have on our mental health and wellbeing. Understanding these effects is essential if we are to take the need for anger management seriously.

Anger, like stress and other powerful emotions, has a profound effect on the body. As our anger rises, the hypothalamus in the brain stimulates the pituitary gland at the base of the skull to release a range of hormones that affect every part of our body in one way or another.

The main hormones are adrenalin and cortisol. Both these hormones exert their influence through the cardiovascular system (the system involving the heart) as well as other systems.

Adrenalin causes the heart to beat faster and the blood pressure to rise; this allows oxygen-rich blood to flow more quickly to the areas of the body responsible for reacting to the source of anger. These areas are those that need extra energy – for example, the arms (to fight) or the legs (to flee) and the brain (to think quickly).

When we are responding to a threat that causes us to get angry, an immediate reaction is required. Blood rushes to the limbs and brain, and is diverted from less important areas of the body like the stomach or skin; now is not the time for the body to be worrying about digestion or maintaining healthy skin. Instead, all resources are diverted to concentrating on dealing with the immediate problem. It is just like a workplace coping with a crisis; all non-essential functions stop while the employees deal with the immediate emergency.

All this anticipated extra activity requires extra energy and the other important hormone, cortisol, is responsible for this bit of the anger reaction. The release of cortisol into the blood causes the liver to convert its emergency stores of energy (in the form of glycogen) into the more readily usable form of glucose. This extra glucose provides the surge of energy needed to beat the source of the anger.

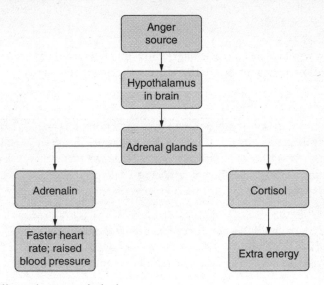

The effects of anger on the body

The net effect of all this activity is a rapid heartbeat, breathlessness (as the lungs struggle to take in more oxygen), raised blood pressure (hypertension) and a raised body temperature (due to using more energy). All this made our angry ancestors ideally placed to deal with the sources of their anger by either fighting their opponent or running away.

Point to remember

Anger causes physical reactions in our body because it was designed to help us fight or flee.

Nowadays, however, these responses are less useful. Rarely do we have the chance to react to the sources of our anger in the way our body was designed to – if we did, we might well find ourselves in trouble with the law. Instead of making use of the extra energy and resources our bodies have provided us with, we are left with all this anger reaction and nowhere to take it. This can leave us with a range of short-term symptoms. Do the following quiz to see if you recognize any of these effects of anger on your body.

When you have been really angry, how much have you experienced the following symptoms (either during the anger episode or afterwards)?

Symptom	1 Never	2 Occasionally	3 Sometimes	4 Quite often	5 Very often
Aching limbs (arms or legs)					
Headache					
Neckache					
Tiredness					
Dry mouth					
Stomachache/ butterflies					
Dizziness					

What your scores mean
The higher your score, the more impact the anger reaction is having on your body. The following table explains why you might experience the symptoms that you do.

Symptom	Why does it occur?
Aching limbs	The build-up of glucose in the limbs can make our arms and legs feel heavy and tired. In addition, we tend to tense our muscles in preparation for flight or fight and this tension causes pain.
Headache	The increased blood supply to the brain, which enables us to think more clearly, may build up pressure, which causes headache.

(*contd*)

Symptom	Why does it occur?
Neckache	We tend to tense our neck muscles when stressed, causing pain.
Tiredness	We feel tired because we have been burning up so much extra energy.
Dry mouth	Flow of saliva to the mouth is reduced.
Stomachache/butterflies	Blood is diverted away from this area so digestive mechanisms are reduced – this can lead to digestive problems and discomfort.
Dizziness	Although we breathe more quickly when we are stressed, we tend to take more shallow breaths and thus we do not breathe in as much oxygen as deeply as when we are not stressed. This can lead to a slightly reduced supply to the brain, causing dizziness.

These are only the short-term effects of anger. If we are chronically angry, i.e. we are angry too often, the repeated activation of the anger system can result in more serious long-term effects, as shown in the following table.

Condition	Reason for its development
Hypertension (raised blood pressure)	This is the result of the heart continually working hard at pumping blood around the body extra quickly.

Condition	Reason for its development
Cardiovascular disease	The increase in blood pressure can damage the delicate lining of some blood vessels. The points where vessels branch into two (branch points) are particularly vulnerable and, if the smooth vessel lining is torn, access to fatty acids and glucose (the production of which increases during the emotional response) is allowed. This causes a build-up of fatty nutrients underneath the tear in the vessel wall. This process gives rise to plaques (lesions) in the blood vessels. These plaques may obstruct the flow of blood to the heart, leading to a heart attack, or to the brain, causing a stroke.
Stomach ulcers	Poor digestion for long periods can result in stomach problems. In addition, there will be excess acid in the stomach, creating conditions in which the bacterium causing stomach ulcers can thrive.
Exhaustion	The rapid mobilization of energy gives short-term benefits but may eventually lead to long-term exhaustion.
Skin disorders	Rashes and allergies can result from the continued decrease of blood to the skin.
Frequent colds or flu	Like stress, chronic anger can result in a lowered immune system, making the person more vulnerable to disease.

If understanding the short-term symptoms of chronic anger is not enough to help us recognize the value of anger management, then perhaps the longer-term consequences as outlined above will be.

> **Quick fix**
> Try making a conscious effort to relax your muscles when you are angry, to reduce some of the uncomfortable effects that anger can produce in your body.

Vicki's story

Vicki, who works in the public sector, used to be a fairly calm person who never lost her temper without good reason. Recently, though, her work has become increasingly stressful; job cuts have meant that although Vicki is lucky enough still to have a job, she is doing the job of two other people who were made redundant in addition to her own.

It is not just the stress of having too much to do that is causing Vicki problems. Customers now have to wait longer for her attention, and so she has to deal with more angry customers. Their anger makes Vicki angry: it's not her fault that they are kept waiting longer. However, most of her anger is directed at management for putting her in this position and not giving her the support she needs. She is also increasingly angry at the Government, which she blames for creating the whole mess in the first place.

The problem is that she can't express her feelings towards these sources of her anger. Instead, she moans to her colleagues and constantly feels wound up like a spring. She is aware that she feels tense all the time and has tightness in her chest. She is also permanently tired and her eczema is worse than usual. Sometimes she wakes in the night and then can't get back to sleep. She goes to her doctor about her eczema and also to see about sleeping tablets. Her doctor discovers that she has very high blood pressure. Vicki knows exactly why.

How anger affects our mental health

Long-term or chronic anger can also affect our mental health and lead to conditions such as anxiety or depression. This is because if we are frequently angry we spend a great deal of our time preoccupied with the source of our anger and what we plan to do about it; we often find ourselves going over and over it in our minds until we are riddled with anxiety.

Chronic anger can also lead us to become depressed, as we are constantly feeling that our rights are being violated and that nothing goes right for us. This can lead to paranoia and the belief that the whole world is against us. If our anger has no real outlet or resolution, this can lead to a condition of **learned helplessness,** which is a precursor to depression. Feeling depressed can then lead to more anger: we feel angry that so many things seem to be going wrong for us and that everything seems to be against us.

> ### Point to remember
>
> Chronic anger can make us depressed as we turn that anger in on ourselves.

The problem escalates because angry people tend to drive people away with their outbursts, resentment and bitterness, which leads to isolation, lack of social support and more depression.

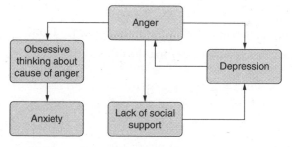

How anger can lead to anxiety and depression

Anger often leads to other emotions, such as hate or humiliation. Indeed, research into chronic anger (Fitness, 2000) suggests that when anger does not have a healthy outlet, it can transform into these other emotional states. This leads on to the issue of whether it is better to express anger or suppress it.

Quick fix
Finding a healthy outlet for your anger can reduce anger's negative effects on your mental health.

'Being' angry can lead to a number of outcomes, and many of these depend on whether you express or suppress that anger. How do you deal with your anger? Do the following quiz to find out whether you are a suppressor or an expresser.

Decide whether the following statements are true or false.

If something makes me really angry I tend to tell my friends about it.	True [1]	False [2]
People around me probably don't know when I am angry.	True [2]	False [1]
When I am angry, I am likely to Facebook/email/text about the incident.	True [1]	False [2]
Telling other people about what has got me angry makes me feel a bit better.	True [1]	False [2]
If I am angry, I tend to keep it to myself.	True [2]	False [1]
I tend to shout and scream when I am angry.	True [1]	False [2]
Other people know when I am angry.	True [1]	False [2]
Being angry often leads to me feeling depressed.	True [2]	False [1]
I don't see any point in shouting the odds when I am angry.	True [2]	False [1]
When I am angry I tend to withdraw into myself.	True [2]	False [1]
I quite often write letters when I am angry.	True [1]	False [2]
I like to think of myself as someone who stays calm even when provoked.	True [2]	False [1]
If someone makes me angry it can take me days before I tell them.	True [2]	False [1]

How to score
Add up the numbers beside your answers. The lower your score (i.e. nearer to 1), the more of an expresser you are, while a higher score means it is more likely that you are a suppressor.

Now that you have an idea of whether you tend to express or suppress your anger, the real question is, which is better? There is evidence suggesting that people who tend to suppress their anger also tend to have high blood pressure (Harburg et al., 1973 and 1979; Gentry et al., 1982) compared with those who express it. The suppression of anger has been considered an important component of the 'hypertensive personality' by many investigators (Pernini et al., 1988; Schneider et al., 1986). Chronically suppressing anger, or 'keeping it in', can thus contribute to coronary heart disease in the long term (Robins and Novaco, 2000); one recent study (Leineweber et al., 2009) showed that men who tended to suppress their anger were up to five times more likely to suffer a heart attack than men who let their anger show.

Point to remember

Suppressing our anger instead of expressing it can lead to higher blood pressure.

Researchers do not understand exactly how or why suppression of anger has these effects. It is thought that anger that simmers and boils below the surface causes a tension that, if not released, causes blood pressure to rise.

Quick fix

If you tend to suppress your anger, try to find healthy ways to express it as much as you can.

If hiding or suppressing our anger is bad for us, is expressing anger a healthier way to deal with being angry? It would certainly seem that anger expressed in a 'positive, assertive and problem-focused' way is healthier than chronic anger suppression (Deffenbacher et al., 1996). Healthier ways to express anger will be discussed in chapter 4.

Our motives for expressing anger can have an impact on whether this expression is healthy or not. For example, if we express anger in order to intimidate or threaten an offender, or because we just can't contain our feelings any longer, this could lead to outbursts with negative consequences. Expressing because we want the other person to know how we feel, on the other hand, or to effect some change, is likely to lead to a healthier outcome.

Similarly, there are a number of reasons for suppression of anger. We may be dealing with someone in a position of power over us (e.g. our boss at work) or it may be because we just don't know how to express the anger appropriately or, indeed, whether we are even entitled to feel angry. These blocks to healthy expression will be dealt with in more detail in chapter 4.

Other consequences of anger

As well as the effects on health that anger can have, there are other, short-term, consequences of anger episodes. These fall into a number of different themes, as shown in the following table.

Theme	Consequence of anger	Explanation of theme/ examples
1	Punishing the person who made us angry	Seeking revenge, spreading gossip or lies about the person, maligning them.
2	Constructive attempt at resolution	Apologizing or accepting an apology, making the first move, trying to negotiate a solution.
3	Displacement of anger	Anger is not expressed at the source (perhaps because of fear of consequences or because such expression is ineffective) but is instead expressed at partner, spouse, pet, etc. Sometimes passive-aggressive behaviour can result where anger is expressed indirectly (sometimes subconsciously) by, for example, 'forgetting' to do something, being late, etc.

Theme	Consequence of anger	Explanation of theme/examples
4	Effect on emotions	These can be positive (you feel better for expressing the anger or getting a resolution) or negative (such as hostility, resentment, depression, frustration, embarrassment about behaviour, guilt about expressing the anger, etc.).
5	Withdrawal	You refuse to speak to the offender or refuse to speak about what has happened.

Myth buster

It is commonly believed that it is better to hide your anger than let it all out and really lose your temper. However, while it is true that losing your temper can have negative repercussions, 'keeping it all in' is not the answer. Anger management is not about learning to quash or 'control' anger but about learning to express anger in healthy ways.

Looking at examples of anger themes

In the following examples, decide which theme the consequences of the anger incident fall into.

1 Allegra is out shopping in a large mall and enjoying the chance to do some retail therapy. After a few hours she has made several purchases and decides to stop to buy a smoothie and a snack at a food outlet. Handing over her credit card, she is surprised to be told that her card has been stopped and she will have to phone the credit card company to get the block lifted. Alarmed, embarrassed and a bit angry, she rings the number from her mobile. She is left hanging for ages but eventually speaks to the operator, who explains to her that her 'unusual activity' has caused the block. Allegra angrily insists that making several purchases in several shops in a shopping mall in her home town is hardly unusual and the man reassures her that the block is lifted. The whole thing takes about ten minutes. She hands over the card again to buy her food but, to her fury, the card is once more rejected. Not having time to go through the whole performance again, she storms out without her food and sets off home. On the journey, a car cuts in front of her and she finds herself stopping her car, getting out and screaming at the offender. A huge row ensues and other car users intervene before things get more out of hand. Shaking, Allegra drives home.

Which theme does the consequence of Allegra's anger fall into?

2 Paul dislikes his wife's brother and his family. His wife, Judy, is well aware of this. He comes home from work one day to find that she has invited her brother and his obnoxious family to stay for the following weekend. Paul is furious – especially because she did this without asking him. After an initial row, Paul storms out and refuses to discuss it any more. For the rest of the week he barely speaks to his wife and when the weekend comes he is quiet and uncommunicative with her brother and his family.

Which theme does the consequence of Paul's anger fall into?

3 Jessica is a nurse working under pressure on a busy hospital ward. She gets on with most of the doctors and consultants but one of them really puts her back up. He treats the nurses like servants, barking out instructions and putting them down in front of patients. This makes Jessica so angry that eventually she loses her temper and throws a glass of water at him. After she has calmed down, she seeks him out and apologizes for throwing the water and tries to explain to him why he makes her so angry and how she feels when he treats the nurses the way he does.

Which theme does the consequence of Jessica's anger fall into?

4 Eoin has a big argument with a colleague at work over the best way to do a piece of work. Chloe insists on doing it her way but Eoin is adamant that her way will cost the company money – and that he will share the blame for this. Chloe refuses to give in and the project goes the way she wants, which leaves Eoin feeling furious. As he predicted, the project goes wrong and their boss has a go at them for wasting company time and money. Eoin tries to explain that it wasn't the way he wanted to do things but Chloe accuses him of lying and makes them share the blame. Eoin is left feeling angry, resentful and hostile – feelings that stay with him and affect his future dealings with Chloe.

Which theme does the consequence of Eoin's anger fall into?

5 **Phoebe** arranges a night out with her friend Rachel, who cancels at the last minute, claiming to be unwell. Phoebe is upset to miss out on their planned evening but is happy to rearrange. A few days later another friend mentions that she saw Rachel out with a man – the very night she stood Phoebe up. Phoebe is furious to have been treated this way and tells all their mutual friends of Rachel's treachery. She also finds out who Rachel's new man is and discovers that she vaguely knows him. Bumping into him, she snidely tells him to be careful because 'Rachel is not what she seems'.

Which theme does the consequence of Phoebe's anger fall into?

Answers

1 Allegra's anger results in theme 3, displacement. She is unable to resolve the source of the anger and that anger spills out on to a different offender.
2 Paul's anger results in theme 5, withdrawal. He is unable to resolve the issue and so withdraws from the whole episode.
3 Jessica's anger falls into theme 2, resolution, as she attempts to resolve the source of her anger.
4 Eoin's anger falls into theme 4, emotions. His anger is converted into different long-term emotions that fester inside him.
5 Phoebe's anger falls into theme 1, punishment. She attempts to get her revenge on Rachel by punishing her for what she did.

Keeping a thematic anger consequence diary

Understanding the themes that the consequences of our anger fall into can help us understand the effects that our anger has on us and on the people around us. Quite often, we find that much of our anger results in similar themes; for example, people prone to withdrawing tend to see this consequence crop up frequently, while individuals prone to displacement will see this theme pop up a lot. Knowing our propensity to react in certain ways can be an important step when it comes to trying to manage our anger to result in more constructive outcomes.

It is useful, then, to record the consequences of any anger episodes you experience by keeping a diary in the form of a chart like this one.

What made you angry?	What was the consequence of your anger?	What theme did that consequence fall into?

Continue charting the consequences of your anger as you progress through the book. You should find that the themes change to more constructive outcomes as you work through the chapters.

Myth buster
It is not true that anger *always* has negative consequences: expressing anger appropriately can lead to the successful resolution of an issue.

How variations in anger episodes produce different effects

Not all incidents of anger will produce the same effects. Anger is not the same in every situation: we experience anger with varying intensity and for different durations. Some researchers believe that the key influence on whether the consequences of anger are bad for you is the *frequency* with which anger is experienced; even mild anger, if felt frequently, can have negative effects on health.

> **Myth buster**
> People often think it is OK to be angry as long as you don't get really angry. This is not true: mild anger experienced frequently can be more damaging than strong but infrequent outbursts.

On the other hand, others claim that frequency is less of a key issue than intensity; our depth of feeling is what really affects the outcomes of angry episodes. According to research (Booth, 2010), people rate most anger incidents as being 'moderate to high' in intensity. This research suggests that the *duration* of anger episodes is what has the biggest impact on our health; anger that lasts longer is more harmful to us than anger that dissipates quickly. Most people feel angry for about five to ten minutes following an anger-inducing episode. However, around 14 per cent of anger incidents lead to angry feelings lasting half a day, with 9 per cent lasting a whole day or even longer. That is a lot of anger washing around, with the resultant physical changes outlined above being present during the entire duration of the episode.

Consequences of anger can also depend upon whether or not the incident is successfully *resolved* – or at least whether the angry person perceives it to be resolved. It would seem that most of our anger episodes are not resolved successfully; one study (Averill, 1982) suggested that only 27 per cent of anger episodes are resolved to the satisfaction of the angry person.

If the anger is not resolved, this can lead to feelings of hostility, a desire for revenge and deep-seated bitterness and resentment, none of which are healthy outcomes.

Gender and anger

Think about the following questions.

▶ Do you think that women get angry as much as men?
▶ Do men express their anger in different ways from women?
▶ Do you think men are more likely to suppress their anger than women?

Our attitudes to anger

Consider this scenario and answer the questions that follow on a scale of 1 to 5, with 1 being not at all and 5 being extremely so.

Sam is at work when a colleague starts to complain that he has not passed on a message from an important client who rang. Sam has no idea what his colleague is talking about and denies all responsibility. The client has not left any message with Sam, who tries to explain this. The colleague is not interested in Sam's explanations and tries to storm off. Sam loses his temper at this and grabs his colleague by the arm and starts shouting loudly. He jabs his finger at his colleague and bangs his fist on the desk. Everyone is starting to stare at the angry outburst.

Question	1	2	3	4	5
How much do you feel that Sam's anger is justified?					
How appropriate do you think Sam's expression of his anger is?					
How effective at his job do you think Sam is?					
How do you rate Sam in terms of his masculinity?					

Now repeat the exercise with the following scenario.

Sam is at work when a colleague starts to complain that she has not passed on a message from an important client who rang. Sam has no idea what her colleague is talking about and denies all responsibility. The client has not left any message with Sam, who tries to explain this. The colleague is not interested in Sam's explanations and tries to storm off. Sam loses her temper at this and grabs her colleague by the arm and starts shouting loudly. She jabs her finger at her colleague and bangs her fist on the desk. Everyone is starting to stare at the angry outburst.

Question	1	2	3	4	5
How much do you feel that Sam's anger is justified?					
How appropriate do you think Sam's expression of her anger is?					
How effective at her job do you think Sam is?					
How do you rate Sam in terms of her femininity?					

Compare your answers. It is likely that you will have given different responses to each set of questions, depending on whether you thought Sam was male or female.

We tend to hold different attitudes towards anger depending on whether the angry person is male or female. In fact, men and women do not differ in how much they get angry or feel angry, but they do differ in how they express their anger. Men are more aggressive in their outbursts – and are also perceived as more aggressive. It is likely that the male Sam in the scenarios above is perceived as being more aggressive than the female Sam. In general, women's anger is viewed more harshly than that of men; we accept men getting angry more readily (and thus might be more likely to rate the male Sam as a more effective worker than the female Sam). Research (Thomas, Smucker and Droppleman, 1998) has suggested that women who express their anger tend to attract more negative labels or descriptions (such as 'cow' or 'bitch') than men.

Another interesting gender difference is that anger tends to enhance masculinity for males but to detract from the femininity of females (Miron-Spektor and Rafaeli, 2009). When women get very angry, they are perceived to have 'lost control', whereas men getting angry are seen to be in control and standing up for their rights. At work, then, men's anger tends to be accepted while angry women are judged to be less competent.

The moral of all this research is that the consequences of being angry are often worse for women than for men. This can lead to more suppression of anger for women than for men, which can lead to more unhealthy outcomes for females.

Jackie's story

Jackie, a manager in a large bank, is finding it increasingly difficult to express her anger appropriately. Recently promoted, she is the only female manager in her branch. The other managers often seem to get angry – when staff members are late for work, when they make mistakes, when they don't show initiative, when they don't pass messages on, etc. – and when they get angry, Jackie notices that their subordinates listen. When the same thing happens to Jackie and she gets angry, all she seems to get are smirks, suppressed laughter and snide comments from her team.

Jackie decides to ask a trusted (male) colleague why she is getting the reaction that she gets – and why it is so different from the reaction that the men get. Her colleague tells her that she is expressing her anger 'like a woman'. He says that when she shouts she sounds like a 'shrieking fishwife', whereas her male colleagues sound assertive. He tells her that her team members consider her to be emotional when she gets angry, whereas her male colleagues are viewed as rational when they get angry. Her anger at them is viewed as a weakness, not as the strength in which her male colleagues' anger seems to be viewed.

Jackie decides that the best way to tackle this is by changing the way she expresses her anger. She lowers her voice to avoid 'shrieking' but, more importantly, she tries to avoid face-to-face confrontation and to express her anger by email or memo instead. These strategies seem to have some effect but she realizes that it is probably not enough. She therefore decides to put in a request to her line manager for the whole team to be given some diversity training with relation to gender and perceptions of anger.

MOVING ON

This chapter has looked at the negative consequences that our anger can have on our body and mind. Understanding the way the anger response works is an important basic step on the road to anger management, especially as, later on, we will be looking at ways to interrupt this response. Understanding the different consequences that anger can have and the factors that influence those consequences is also vital in ensuring we can take full, informed responsibility for our actions. The 'angry personality' – in terms of both getting angry and the outcomes of that anger – will be introduced in the next chapter.

Key points

1 The response that anger produces in our bodies is normal, even though it leads to unhealthy consequences.

2 Recording and coding the consequences of your anger episodes as you continue through this book will help with charting your progress in your anger management skill development.

3 Anger can have both short- and long-term effects on your body and mind, and this chapter has helped you to start being more aware of these.

4 Different anger episodes can lead to different outcomes but, quite often, we have our own typical outcomes to anger incidents.

5 The consequences of being angry are often worse for women than for men, which can lead women to suppress their anger, with unhealthy outcomes for them.

3

....

Do you have a problem with your anger?

How do you feel?
Answer 'true' or 'false' to the following statements.

- *I lose my temper too often.   T/F*
- *I feel that I am always angry.   T/F*
- *I am often disappointed in life.   T/F*
- *There seem to be so many things that make me angry.   T/F*
- *Annoying things happen to me a lot.   T/F*

According to the Mental Health Foundation (2008), more than one in four of us worry about how angry we sometimes feel. If you answered 'true' to any of these statements, you may well have a problem with your anger and even what is termed an 'angry personality'. This chapter explains how to diagnose and manage the angry personality.

_____

Is your anger a problem?

Anger can be a problem for a number of reasons. To see if your anger is a problem for you, answer the questions in the following quiz by stating how much you agree with each of the statements.

	4 Strongly agree	3 Agree	2 Disagree	1 Strongly disagree
I lose my temper a lot.				
It doesn't take much to get me angry.				

(*contd*)

	4 Strongly agree	3 Agree	2 Disagree	1 Strongly disagree

I feel angry all the time.

I have a short fuse.

I feel irritable a lot.

I get very angry very quickly.

When I am angry I feel out of control.

I tend to complain about other people a lot.

I often feel bitter or resentful.

People often tell me to calm down.

I shout when I am angry.

I get aggressive when I am angry.

I often slam doors or other objects when I am angry.

I fly into a rage quite easily.

I take my anger out on my partner or kids.

I am angrier than I used to be.

I worry about really losing it.

How to interpret your score
The higher the score, the more your anger is a problem for you.
Scores bigger than 50 indicate more serious anger problems. High
scores mean that either you are angry too often, experience anger
too intensely or express it inappropriately.

'I am constantly angry and when it builds up there is no way out
but being aggressive. When the wave of anger starts I lose myself
in it. I don't seem to know myself any more and my friends and
family are concerned for their and my safety. My bursts usually
end up with blood because to avoid anything serious I usually
punch the wall. I have had a wall cave in. My anger seems to
take over the whole time.'

Post on Yahoo Answers, 2009

Why anger can be a problem

Until now the assumption has been that anger is only a problem
when there is too much of it, when it is too intense or when it is
expressed inappropriately. However, anger can be a problem for
other reasons too, including:

▶ not getting angry enough
▶ not feeling able to express anger
▶ not knowing when we are entitled to feel anger.

These are likely to be an issue for you if you agree with more than
four of the following statements:

Statement	Agree	Disagree
I am very laid back and rarely get angry.		
Nothing really gets me angry.		
I don't get angry because I never really feel that there is anything worth getting angry about.		
People tend not to treat me unfairly.		
Life is pretty fair, really.		

(contd)

If I am treated badly I just shrug it off.

Getting angry doesn't win you friends.

No one likes a Mr or Ms Angry.

My 'rights' aren't really that important to me.

I am never really sure if I ought to be angry.

I usually look to other people to see if something is worth getting angry about.

If I feel angry I ask my partner if they think it is worth getting angry about.

I am afraid of the consequences of getting angry.

Myth buster
Anger isn't just a problem when there is too much of it; not getting angry enough can indicate anger issues too.

If you agree with the statements above it is likely that your anger is not as under control as you might think; in fact, your lack of anger is because you are being passive and not standing up for yourself. This might mean that you are being taken advantage of and that you are losing out in other ways because of your slowness to anger. This will be dealt with more in chapter 4.

Harry's story

Harry considers himself to be a calm person and others also think of him as a person who has a calming influence and who never gets angry. He works hard in a bank and has a wife and three lovely children. Life in the bank is stressful and, although he would love nothing more than to come home and relax, he knows that he will come home to find the breakfast things still on the table and no supper being prepared. His wife works part-time and is quite a tense person who gets angry over the slightest thing.

Harry's strategy has always been to go for the easy life. He lets his wife scream at him and he accepts the children not lifting a finger to help, just for the sake of peace. At work, too, he often feels put upon but is afraid to rock the boat by complaining – anyway, what's the point? Getting angry will just mean shouting and losing his temper, which creates more stress and hostility. It's easier just to take it and keep his head down.

In addition, Harry is never sure whether he ought to get angry about things or not. Sometimes, over a pint in the pub, he tells his pals about the cleaning he has just done, the supper he has prepared and the extra work he has done at the bank for no extra pay – and they can't believe that he is putting up with it all. When his friends say this, he thinks that maybe he shouldn't be putting up with so much. But then he goes home or back to work and his courage fails him. He can't help wondering what might happen if he did get angry – maybe he would lose his job; maybe his wife would walk out. After all, no one likes angry people. It's better just to keep his head down and get on with things.

The angry personality

Is there such a thing as an 'angry personality'? Consider the following questions:

▶ Do you know some people who seem to get angry very quickly?
▶ Do some people seem to be constantly angry?
▶ Do you know people around whom you have to 'tread on eggshells' in case they get angry?

The chances are that we all know someone who fits this description – or it may even describe ourselves! If you scored highly in the quiz at the start of this chapter then the chances are that you are Mr or Ms Angry. Having an angry personality means that you are just more likely to get angry than other people. Such people are more 'threat sensitive' than others; they are more likely to perceive a range of stimuli as being a threat to their sense of justice, fairness or wellbeing. They need little provocation to flare up and 'lose it' when the slightest thing affronts them.

Luke's story

Luke works in a highly pressured retail environment. He likes to think that he doesn't stand for any nonsense. He has high expectations of himself and of other people and is intolerant of other people's mistakes. He checks and double-checks everything and expects his staff to do the same. He is happy to admit that he flares up easily when people let him down and he acknowledges that this spills over into his private life too; his flare-ups are legendary with his mates and at home. However, he believes that this is the only way to make sure that no one treats him like dirt – you have to stand up for yourself.

Lately, though, he feels as if his anger has been getting out of control. He seems to 'lose it' at the slightest provocation. It's as if his anger threshold has been lowered so that more and more things make him angry. He is angry at his staff for not doing things the way he would like them done, he is angry at senior management for imposing unrealistic budget cuts, he is angry at his wife for not understanding the pressure he is under. He is often angry with his children's school for various things: letters asking for school trip money; the way they confiscated his youngest's toy; the detention they gave his oldest son. He is often angry with his children, too: for the way they answer back; the way they don't clear the table; the state in which they leave their rooms.

One day he hears a colleague refer to him behind his back as Mr Angry. This makes him stop and think but he isn't unduly concerned until he receives a birthday card from his daughter. In it, the four-year-old has drawn a picture of a big red head with the mouth wide open. When he asks her if that is really him, his daughter replies, 'Yes, that's how you look – your mouth is always open 'cos you are always angry and you are always red in the face.'

Luke knows now that it is time to take stock.

Psychologists have identified some of the personality traits that lead to the angry personality, with one group of researchers identifying what they referred to as 'trait anger' (Forgays et al., 1997). Trait anger differs from 'state anger' in that it refers to a propensity to get angry, rather than a normal reaction to an anger-inducing event. Interestingly, high trait anger people tend not only to get angry more quickly, but seem more capable of processing anger-related information (Martin, Watson and Wan, 2000); this means that they may be more attuned to picking up on anger-eliciting cues. In other words, they are primed to get angrier.

The good news for people with an angry personality is that this trait can be worked on and can change; angry people can become much calmer, slower to anger and more able to withstand provocation. To make this personality change, we need to focus on three main areas:

1 Cognitive factors: how you think
2 Affective factors: how you feel
3 Behavioural factors: how you act

In chapter 1 we discussed the main themes that cause us to become angry, such as frustrations, irritations, abuse and injustice. These are external events and, on their own, do not necessarily cause us to get angry. This is why, when exposed to the same 'anger-inducing' events, some people will remain calm, some will become a bit annoyed and others will become hot with rage. The reason for the differences in these responses has to be tied in with the factors internal to ourselves.

These internal factors reflect individual differences between people and are often linked closely to our personality. It is our inherent personality that is the reason some of us are slow to anger and others are easy to provoke. These personality traits are to do with the ways in which we think, feel and behave and are often learned through exposure to particular events or experiences. These 'prototypical' ways of responding that we have learned have become ingrained, but, with some effort, they can be changed.

Myth buster

Many people think that you cannot change personality, so an angry person will always be angry. This is not true, however: we *can* modify elements of our personality but it does take time and effort to do so.

Cognitive factors

Cognitive factors that can contribute to an angry personality refer to our mental processes, or how we think or process information. These include:

▶ the expectations that we have of the world
▶ our interpretation of events around us.

We will deal with each of these in turn.

OUR EXPECTATIONS OF THE WORLD

Ask yourself the following questions:

▶ Do you have high standards for service in restaurants?
▶ Do you expect high levels of professionalism from your co-workers?
▶ Are you taken aback by setbacks?
▶ Do you tend to underestimate how much traffic will be on the roads when you have to get somewhere?
▶ Are you surprised when you are kept waiting?
▶ Do other people disappoint you a lot?
▶ Do you expect others always to be on time?
▶ Do you expect other people not to make mistakes?
▶ Do you have high expectations of your children?
▶ Do you consider yourself a perfectionist?

The more 'yeses' that you have given to the above questions, the more you may have unrealistic expectations of the world. And the more unrealistic the expectations are that you hold, the more likely you are to get angry when you feel your expectations haven't been met.

The reality is that life does let us down sometimes. Things do not always go as planned; setbacks and delays are inevitable. People who are not realistic enough to accept these are setting themselves up for disappointment – and disappointed people can get angry. Poor service at a restaurant makes them angry, traffic hold-ups make them furious, waiting for the doctor to see them enrages them and other people making mistakes is inordinately frustrating for them.

Quick fix
Try lowering your expectations of the world in order to start managing your anger. Accept that things do go wrong sometimes and life does let you down.

How do we know, though, whether our expectations are too high? Surely it is good to have high standards and expectations? The acid test is probably that if you are constantly disappointed and irritated by other people or events failing to meet your expectations, then holding such high expectations is probably not healthy for you. If lowering your general expectations in life will help you manage your anger, this is a trade-off that might be worth accepting (but don't let your expectations get too low – more on this in chapter 4).

OUR INTERPRETATION OF EVENTS

Events are only anger-inducing if we appraise them or interpret them to be so. We have to perceive something to be a cause of anger before we can feel angry. This is why angry people are often told they are taking things too personally or are too threat-sensitive. The reason that some people interpret events in anger-eliciting ways is partly to do with the expectations they have of the world (see above) and partly to do with the **negative cognitive mindsets** that they hold. These are the negative and typical ways that we have learned to interpret events that happen to us; this is why, for example, one person can take the weather quite personally ('It always rains when I am going somewhere nice – life is so unfair!') while another person accepts the event more objectively ('You can't win them all – last time I went out for the day it was glorious!').

Quick fix

Try not to take things too personally. When something goes wrong, catch any negative thoughts you might have about this 'always happening to me' or being 'typical'.

'THOUGHT-CATCHING'

Now that you have started keeping a diary to record the sources of your anger (see chapter 1) and the consequences of your anger episodes (see chapter 2), the next step is to start examining your thoughts, or the cognitive factors associated with anger episodes. 'Thought-catching' is a way of focusing attention on the cognitive processes in your head – the sort of thoughts that normally barely reach your conscious awareness. Learning to become consciously aware of what is going on in your mind is an important part of the process of discovering what is feeding your anger.

For the thought-catching exercise, all you need to do is to record what you are thinking when you get angry. Use a template like the one below to work though over the next week or so, to record all the times that you find yourself getting angry, as with the example shown.

Thought-catching record sheet

The anger episode: what happened?	What thoughts were going through your mind?
The computer was being really slow and then it wouldn't let me get online at all.	This always happens – it isn't right that I should have to waste so much time just trying to get online. It's my husband's fault – he should have fixed this.

Once you are able to get your thoughts down on paper, you might start to notice patterns to your thinking – these are your cognitive mindsets. For example, you might notice that you are interpreting things too negatively or taking them too personally, or perhaps blaming things too much on other people (or yourself). That would be your cognitive mindset.

Once you start to identify your cognitive mindsets, you need to begin to look at changing the way you typically think. Very often, we slip into our 'prototypical' way of thinking without even being conscious of it; your thought-catching diary will help you become more aware of the flawed cognitive processes that might be fuelling your anger.

Change the way you think by looking back at your thought-catching diary and asking yourself the following questions:

▶ Could I have interpreted the event differently?
▶ Could I be more objective when anger-eliciting events happen?
▶ Could I reframe negative thoughts into more positive ones?

Much of the change that you will need to effect involves transforming the negative cognitive mindsets or thoughts into more positive ones. This is sometimes called **cognitive restructuring** and involves restructuring or reshaping your common, 'prototypical' ways of thinking. Once you are in the habit of catching your negative or unhelpful thoughts (sometimes called 'cognitive distortions'), you can start learning to replace them with more positive or helpful ones.

Quick fix

Try to look at different ways that anger-eliciting events can be interpreted. Before you get angry, look for alternative explanations for what has happened so that you are not always seeing things as personal attacks.

The following sections will help you identify cognitive distortions and suggest ways of replacing them with more helpful interpretations.

OVERCOMING COGNITIVE DISTORTIONS

Five common cognitive distortions are outlined below, along with suggestions for how to overcome them; you might recognize them from your thought-catching record sheet or diary above.

1 Exaggeration

This is when you view things as being worse than they actually are – or you imagine that disastrous or terrible things will result from relatively minor events. If we magnify the significance of things going wrong or bad things happening to us, they are more likely to make us angry.

Exaggeration can also occur inadvertently when we tell other people about what has happened to us. Our friends are likely to side with us and agree that we have been terribly wronged but this can add weight to the body of evidence we have that we have been badly wronged, and can stoke up our anger further.

Another form of exaggeration is when we always see anger-eliciting events as having the same strength in terms of disastrous consequences. Thus, everything that goes wrong is a 'nightmare' or 'disastrous' and makes us 'furious'; there is no middle ground, when events make us 'annoyed' or are 'a bit irritating'.

Here is an example of how we might exaggerate the importance of events.

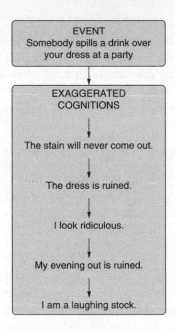

Exaggerations then need to be caught and reframed by challenging the cognitions; is this really a disaster? Could there be less catastrophic consequences? Is it really a 'nightmare'? The above event could thus be reframed in the following way:

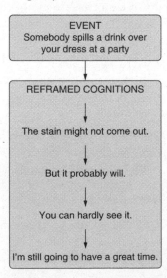

2 Generalization

This is when we fail to see an anger-eliciting event in isolation but try (erroneously) to generalize it to other events in our lives. Common thoughts associated with generalization include: 'This always happens to me', or 'Typical – no one ever shows me respect'. Consider the same example of the spilled drink, but applying the cognitive distortion of generalization:

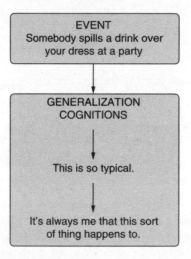

You can challenge generalization cognitive distortions by examining the evidence and remembering the incidents that haven't gone badly. When we are feeling negative or angry, the theory of 'emotional memory' states that we tend to remember other events associated with the same emotions – which mean when we feel angry we remember other times when we were angry. It is thus much harder to recall events that made us happy when we are feeling negative.

> **Point to remember**
>
> When things go wrong for us, it is so easy to generalize these so that it feels as though things are always going wrong. Challenging this belief will help keep anger under control.

The example above could be challenged in the following way.

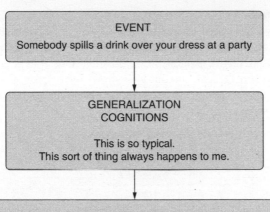

3 Irrationality

Many of our cognitions, or the thoughts that pop into our brain when we are angry, are irrational in that there is no evidence to support them. We might feel angry because we feel that we are the only person that this has ever happened to or that we are special in that we have no right to be treated this badly – we are much too deserving of respect to be treated in such a manner. These irrational thoughts fuel our anger.

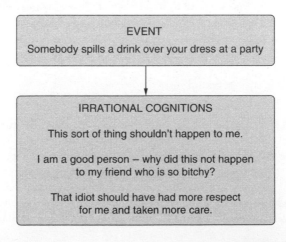

We can challenge irrational thoughts by examining the evidence to support our cognitions, as in the following example.

EVENT

Somebody spills a drink over your dress at a party

IRRATIONAL COGNITIONS

This sort of thing shouldn't happen to me.

I am a good person – why did this not happen to my friend who is so bitchy?

That idiot should have had more respect for me and taken more care.

What is my evidence?

Why shouldn't it happen to me – it's just bad luck and could happen to anyone.

It is irrational to imagine that drunk people are only going to spill drinks on 'bad' people.

He should have had more respect for people but it is irrational to think he should have had any special respect for me.

4 Filtering

This is when we select out and focus on just the negative aspects of a situation, ignoring any positive aspects. This is a common feature of the angry personality. For example, you may have had a great day but you focus only on the event that 'ruins' your day, ignoring all the things that went right. Thus, with the example we are using about the spilled drink, filtering is when the 'victim' ignores the fact that their night out has been great until now or they ignore all the positive elements of the evening that still lie ahead; for example, 'It's not as if I've been hurt or am ill – I can still enjoy the rest of the evening', or 'I'm still here with my friends so can still have fun'.

To counter the filtering cognitions, then, you need to try to refocus on the things that have gone well and try to keep the frustrating event in perspective.

> **Point to remember**
>
> When we are angry, we tend to remember only other things that have made us angry. By trying to focus on positive things that have happened in the past, you can overcome this memory bias that feeds your anger.

5 Misattribution

Many angry people are quick to make negative and 'egocentric' attributions about events that less angry people probably wouldn't. That is, they mistakenly take things too personally and view events as a deliberate and personal attack, as the example below shows.

Counter such misattributions by trying to replace such personal attributions of blame with more general possibilities such as, 'He clearly didn't target me. I was just in the wrong place at the wrong time.'

REPLACING NEGATIVE COGNITIONS
WITH POSITIVE ONES

Go back now to the thought-catching diary that you completed earlier in this chapter. Your task is to use it to transform the negative thoughts to more positive ones, as in the example shown.

Anger-inducing event	Negative thoughts/ cognitive distortions	New, positive interpretation
The computer was being really slow and then it wouldn't let me get online at all.	This always happens – it isn't right that I should have to waste so much time just trying to get online. It's my husband's fault – he should have fixed this.	When this happens I tend to remember all the other times that my computer has crashed – and I forget about the times it works perfectly well. I am wasting time but that is just the way life is sometimes. It happens to everyone – I bet if I ask my friends, computer problems are probably the one thing that really frustrates them all. And my husband hasn't done this deliberately to make me angry.

Quick fix

A really effective way of becoming less angry is to become less stressed and tense. Learn relaxation techniques (see chapter 6) to enable you to do this.

Affective factors

Affective factors are to do with how we feel rather than how we think. Two main interrelated affective contributors can contribute to the angry personality. These are:

▶ **Levels of tension**

People who are generally more tense, anxious or stressed are more easily provoked. When we are tense, it does not take as much to send us over the edge as when we are relaxed. Minor setbacks are seen as catastrophes and small irritations become major grievances. This is why we tend to be slower to anger when we are nice and relaxed on holiday – but lose our cool easily in the airport on the way when we are stressed and anxious. (For more on 'plane rage', see chapter 10.)

▶ **Taking things too seriously**

We have already discussed the issue of taking things too personally (which is part of cognitive distortions), but taking things too seriously is linked to levels of tension. When we are tense and stressed, we tend to take things too seriously and may be unable to distance ourselves enough to put things in perspective. We may find that we don't laugh as much as we used to or seem to have lost our sense of humour altogether. Things that we may have laughed at or shrugged off now make us angry instead.

Are you stressed?

Read the following statements and indicate on a scale of 1 to 5 how much each of them has applied to you over the last three months.

Statement	1 Very infrequently	2 Infrequently	3 Sometimes	4 Frequently	5 Very frequently
I eat more – or less – than usual.					
I suffer from indigestion or heartburn.					

(contd)

Statement	1 Very infrequently	2 Infrequently	3 Sometimes	4 Frequently	5 Very frequently
I suffer from constipation, stomachaches, diarrhoea or other stomach problems.					
I suffer from sleep problems, e.g. difficulty getting to sleep or waking early.					
I feel tired or exhausted.					
I have headaches.					
I feel like crying or as if I might 'explode'.					
I can't sit still without fidgeting, or I pace the floor.					
I feel my blood pressure rising.					
I get impatient or irritable easily.					
I feel unable to cope.					
I have difficulty making decisions.					
I have difficulty concentrating.					
I move on to the next task before completing the present task.					
I smoke or drink more alcohol than I used to.					

(contd)

Statement	1 Very infrequently	2 Infrequently	3 Sometimes	4 Frequently	5 Very frequently
I worry about so many things.					
I feel tense, not relaxed.					
I feel that I don't have time for anything.					
I feel panicky or fearful.					
I feel more irritated than I ought to by interruptions or minor distractions.					

How to interpret your score
The higher your score the more likely it is that you are stressed.
A score above 60 indicates high stress, while one of between 21
and 59 indicates mild stress. A score of 20 or below indicates that
you have low stress levels.

The key to managing these affective factors is relaxation. Techniques
to address this will be discussed in chapter 6.

Point to remember

Managing your stress is an important factor in reducing your
angry personality.

Behavioural factors

Behavioural factors refer to the things we do or the way we behave.
We all tend to develop stereotypical or 'prototypical' ways of
responding to events. Sometimes, these typical responses are referred
to as scripts. This is why we often know pretty much how other people
will react to certain events – we know their typical response pattern.

There are two general styles of behaviour that can contribute towards the angry personality: the avoidance response and the hostility response.

The avoidance response
This is when the individual does not deal with the conflict but withdraws and walks away. We talked about this as a possible consequence of an anger episode in chapter 2; walking away or withdrawing might seem like a good option because it appears to avoid conflict and might thus seem to be a peaceful response but, in reality, it is actually a passive response that can result in negative outcomes:

▶ The conflict remains unresolved.
▶ The anger remains.
▶ The passive response can impair our self-worth and self-esteem.

Anger that is not directed outwards can easily be directed inwards towards ourselves, leading to depression or other emotional problems (see chapter 2).

The hostility response
This is when a person typically reacts with hostility or aggression to provocation. People with the 'hostile script' ingrained in them flare up quickly and become aggressive rapidly. Such scripts are rarely effective in achieving much, since many people react to hostility and aggression by becoming hostile and aggressive themselves. This leads to a cycle of hostility and aggression, with each person's hostility adding to the anger cycle.

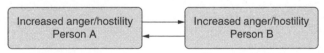

The cycle of hostility

Point to remember

When you get angry, you are likely to get into an anger cycle with the other person, causing the anger to escalate. Break the cycle by toning down your hostility.

An effective way to tackle the hostility script is using the more assertive scripts that will be discussed in the next chapter.

MOVING ON

This chapter has been concerned with the angry personality and the results of the self-assessment tests should have given you a good idea of whether anger is a problem for you. We have started to look at the three main ways (cognitive, affective and behavioural) in which the angry personality is maintained so that we can break down these factors and start making our personality a little less anger-prone.

Key points

1 Anger can be a problem for you if there is too much of it, if it is expressed inappropriately or if it is felt too intensely – but anger can also be a problem for people who rarely get angry.

2 Changing our view of the world can really influence how anger-prone we are; people with high expectations of the world are less tolerant of things going wrong and so get angry when they do.

3 People who make cognitive distortions when they interpret events around them are more likely to be anger-prone.

4 Breaking habitual ways of responding to anger-eliciting events can help interrupt the anger cycle and stop it escalating.

5 People who are stressed and tense are more likely to get angry; learning to relax and manage stress is an effective way to lower general sensitivity to anger-inducing events.

How to express anger appropriately

How do you feel?
Answer 'true' or 'false to the following statements.

- *I sometimes feel unsure about whether I ought to be getting angry or not.*   T/F
- *I know I probably get a bit aggressive sometimes when I am angry.*   T/F
- *I am not sure how to express my anger in an appropriate way.*   T/F
- *I feel I could be more assertive when complaining about things.*   T/F
- *When I get angry I can often feel things getting out of control.*   T/F

According to the Mental Health Foundation (2008), one in five people say that they have ended a relationship or friendship with someone because of how they behaved when they were angry. If you answered 'true' to any of the above statements, this chapter will help you with the issues raised. It will tell you how to know when you are entitled to get angry and when you are not, how to avoid coming across as aggressive and how to express your anger assertively.

Know when you are right to feel angry

What rights do you think you (and other people) have in terms of anger? Write down as many as you can think of (but cover up the list that follows first!). For example, you might write, 'I have the right to feel angry if someone treats me badly.'

Compare your list to the list below:

EXERCISE

- ▶ I have the right to feel angry if someone treats me badly.
- ▶ I have the right to express my opinion.
- ▶ I have the right to disagree with other people.
- ▶ I have the right to say no.
- ▶ I have the right to feel angry.
- ▶ I have the right to ask for what I want.
- ▶ I have the right to be treated with respect.
- ▶ I have the right to fair and just treatment.
- ▶ I have the right to make mistakes.
- ▶ I have the right not to be taken for granted.
- ▶ I have the right to think of myself sometimes.
- ▶ I have the right not to be put upon.
- ▶ I have the right to a fair workload.
- ▶ I have the right to protest against unfair criticism.
- ▶ I have the right not to be shouted at.

Of course, in being aware of your rights to feel and be angry, you have to recognize that other people have these rights too and thus, when you are expressing anger, it is important to do so in a way that does not violate the rights of other people.

The right to be angry

Usually, anger manifests itself in one of three ways. The first is outward expressions of anger, which include shouting, screaming or even violence, and even less threatening approaches like sarcasm. Inward expressions of anger are those occasions when we bottle it up by seething, biting our tongue or hiding our angry feelings. Neither of these approaches is healthy. The third way to express anger is by appropriate expression, which will be the focus of this chapter. Before we can examine such techniques, it is vital that you understand and accept your right to be angry.

Myth buster
Keeping a 'lid' on your anger is not healthy and is not the aim of anger management programmes.

As mentioned previously, anger management is not about eliminating anger or trying to stop its expression. On the contrary, healthy expression of anger is an essential part of normal functioning and people with 'anger issues' can include those individuals who suppress their anger as well as those who express it inappropriately. The first step, then, is to write down the 'rights' that you have in terms of anger.

Point to remember

Anger management is not about stopping you feeling or expressing your anger on those occasions when you have every right to be angry.

Quick fix

An important part of the process of anger management is recognizing when you are entitled to be angry and when you are not.

Other people's rights

Using the list of rights above, write the corresponding 'right' that other people have. The first one is done for you.

My rights	Other people's rights
I have the right to feel angry if someone treats me badly.	Other people also have the right to feel angry if I treat them badly.
I have the right to express my opinion.	
I have the right to disagree with other people.	
I have the right to say no.	
I have the right to feel angry.	
I have the right to ask for what I want.	
I have the right to be treated with respect.	
I have the right to fair and just treatment.	

(*contd*)

EXERCISE

My rights	Other people's rights

I have the right to make mistakes.

I have the right not to be taken for granted.

I have the right to think of myself sometimes.

I have the right not to be put upon.

I have the right to a fair workload.

I have the right to protest against unfair criticism.

I have the right not to be shouted at.

The right to be angry (and the right of other people to be angry) lies at the heart of being assertive. However, it is important also to be aware of what your rights do not mean; i.e. when you are *not* entitled to be angry. For example:

▶ I do not have the automatic right to get angry when other people make mistakes.

▶ I do not have the right to get angry because other people don't do what I want.

▶ I do not have the right to get angry because other people's opinions differ from mine.

▶ I do not have the right to get angry because other people disagree with me.

Expressing anger appropriately means expressing it in an assertive manner. People who are not assertive are either too passive (leading to too much suppression and/or negative effects on self-esteem) or too aggressive (leading to too much inappropriate expression). People who are too passive are not aware or accepting enough of their own rights, while people who are too aggressive are not aware enough or accepting of the rights of other people.

Danielle is in a long-term relationship with Ben. She begins to find that she is often angry with him, feeling that he is taking her for granted and no longer making much of an effort for her. She thinks he seems to believe he can just click his fingers and she will come running. He cancels dates at the last minute and sometimes does not even turn up, but when he is at a loose end he calls her at short notice and expects her to drop everything and go out with him.

Danielle is getting increasingly resentful but, whenever she tries to tell Ben how she feels, he always seems to have an answer. He says he is entitled to go out with his own friends, some of whom he has known for years. He feels it is entirely reasonable to put them first sometimes and that they would do the same for him.

Danielle feels confused about whether she is being unreasonable and too demanding. Her own friends tell her that she is entitled to be treated better but she isn't sure any more. Maybe Ben is right and being a loyal friend is more important than spending time with her.

Then Danielle sees a 'bill of rights' on the Internet and begins to realize that Ben is in fact violating many of her rights. She recognizes that while Ben has the right to choose who to spend his time with, she also has the right to be treated with respect – and that means not being constantly let down at the last minute. She also has the right not to be taken for granted and realizes that, in allowing Ben to do this, she is effectively saying that his rights (to do as he wants) are more important than hers (to do as she wants).

Feeling more confident now that she is entitled to be angry about the situation, Danielle calmly explains to Ben that his behaviour is no longer acceptable. As usual, he says that it is she who is being unreasonable. Danielle realizes that she isn't going to change him and so she ends the relationship.

Quick fix
While it is important to know that you have rights, accepting that other people have rights too is a way to reduce aggressive expressions of anger.

Standing up for your rights

You are being assertive when you stand up for these rights, but in such a way as to recognize the rights of others. Thus part of being assertive is to accept that others have the same rights. People generally use one of three interpersonal styles with regard to asserting their rights: passive, aggressive and assertive.

THE PASSIVE STYLE

This is when people fail to express their rights adequately, perhaps because they cannot really accept that they have the same rights as other people (often due to low self-esteem). Passive people find it hard to say no; they do things they do not want to do because they feel that other people are more important than they are and have a greater right to assert themselves. They find it hard to put themselves first, hard to stand up for themselves when criticized and feel that they must always please others.

Such people may feel frustrated at being so passive and this style can adversely affect their self-esteem. Passive people find it hard to express their anger and are constantly preoccupied with wondering whether they are entitled to be angry in a given situation and, if so, how to express that anger without causing offence. At work, this might mean that they are likely to be given the unpopular jobs, to take too much on and to find it hard to stand up to the boss or co-workers.

THE AGGRESSIVE STYLE

Here, people are well aware of their own rights, but often express them in a way that violates the rights of others. It can be a confrontational style that rides roughshod over people's feelings. Such people come across as arrogant and superior and they can even seem frightening or threatening (especially to more passive friends or colleagues). They are less worried about pleasing other people or about the impression they create than they are about making sure that they are not being treated as 'doormats'.

Aggressive people are usually very good at expressing their anger but do so in a manner that wins enemies, not friends. The aggressive style is rarely acceptable at work (although that depends on the organizational culture as some are more tolerant of this style than others), or beyond work, and aggression that appears to be or is threatening is likely to attract disciplinary or legal consequences.

THE ASSERTIVE STYLE

People who express their rights assertively do so in a way that ensures that they know their own rights as well as those of other people. They accept that they cannot please everyone all the time and that sometimes they will have to put their own needs first. At the same time, they realize that other people have an equal right to want to put their own needs first and to say no to any requests if they wish. Assertive people are able to express their anger when it is appropriate to do so but in a way that is not threatening to others.

Passive, aggressive or assertive?

Read the following scenario and the three responses to it. Decide in each case whether Kyle is being passive, aggressive or assertive.

> Kyle is shopping in his local supermarket. When he finishes, he pushes his trolley to a till but finds that another shopper has loaded their shopping on to the conveyer belt but then abandoned it and their trolley, presumably while they go back to look for a missing item. Which of the following responses of Kyle's is passive, which is aggressive and which assertive?

Response 1: Kyle shoves all the loaded items into the empty trolley and pushes the trolley out of the way before starting to load his own stuff. As he does so, the missing shopper returns and angrily exclaims that he was here first and only nipped back to swap an item with a longer shelf life. Kyle says 'Tough!' and carries on, but the other shopper starts trying to load his shopping too and the consequence is that a physical standoff of pushing and shoving ensues.

Passive   Aggressive   Assertive

Response 2: Kyle waits patiently for the missing shopper to return. When he does return, the other shopper ignores Kyle and carries on with paying and loading his shopping.

Passive   Aggressive   Assertive

Response 3: Kyle waits a short time for the shopper to return. When he doesn't, he then moves his trolley to the front and starts handing his items directly to the cashier to be scanned. As he is doing this, the errant shopper returns and starts demanding to know why Kyle is 'pushing in'. Kyle calmly states that 'You weren't here so I have carried on – I won't be long now,' and continues to get his shopping scanned. The angry shopper huffs and puffs but Kyle stands his ground and makes no further response.

Passive   Aggressive   Assertive

Discovering your typical response pattern

Before moving on to look at developing assertive anger scripts to replace passive or aggressive ones, it is useful at this stage to diagnose your typical response pattern to see if it is passive or aggressive. The following quiz will help achieve this.

Are you passive or aggressive?

Use the scale to indicate your strength of agreement or disagreement with each statement.

Statement	1 Strongly disagree	2 Disagree	3 Neither agree nor disagree	4 Agree	5 Strongly agree
I am often unsure whether I am entitled to be angry or not.					
I often suppress my anger.					
I always seem to be letting off steam at home.					
I am not afraid to show my anger.					

Statement	1 Strongly disagree	2 Disagree	3 Neither agree nor disagree	4 Agree	5 Strongly agree
There are some people who really intimidate me.					
I am afraid to show my anger.					
People would be disappointed in me if I became angry.					
I point at people a lot when I am angry.					
People often tell me to calm down.					
People often seem to be backing away from me when I am angry.					
It is really important to me that everyone likes me.					

How to interpret your score
'Passive' score: This is your total score for items 1, 2, 5, 6, 7 and 11. Scores over 24 indicate that this is your dominant style.

'Aggressive' score: This is your total score for items 3, 4, 8, 9, 10. Scores over 20 indicate that this is your dominant style.

If you have a passive or dominant style in relation to your expression of anger, you will need to start learning to transfer this into a more assertive style of anger expression. Being assertive when you are angry means recognizing when your rights have been violated, allowing you to acknowledge your anger and expressing that anger assertively when it is appropriate to do so – and without violating the rights of other people. Expressing anger assertively is a learned skill that involves the use of both assertive anger scripts and assertive language. Both of these are discussed in the next sections.

Assertive anger scripts

When we get angry, we tend to revert to 'prototypical' ways of reacting – these are sometimes called scripts. Learning to adopt assertive anger scripts will help you develop a more effective way of expressing your anger – without being either too passive or aggressive. Your script should contain the key elements set out in the following table.

Quick fix

Changing the way you typically respond to anger-inducing situations from using passive or aggressive scripts to more assertive ones will help you express your anger more appropriately.

Assertive anger script element	Examples
Begin (and end) on a positive note.	'I know you're only trying to help but...' 'I know you do care about my child's welfare and I've had no problems before, but...'
Define the problem specifically and early; don't prevaricate by taking ages to get to the point.	'I really feel you've not shown that you understand the issues I'm having here.' 'I feel you've shown me disrespect by using the language that you've just used...'
Use the first person to avoid statements of blame.	'I feel angry' rather than 'You make me angry'; 'I feel hurt' rather than 'You have upset me.'

Assertive anger script element	Examples
Explain how you feel.	'I feel worried about my job security when I'm not kept informed about organizational changes.' 'I'm concerned that you will think this is a petty matter, but...'
Don't put yourself down.	'I'm probably being too sensitive...' 'Perhaps it's just me...'
Focus on the main issue and don't get sidetracked on to past grievances.	'While we're on the subject...' 'Something similar happened six months ago too...'
Do criticize the behaviour and not the person.	'I felt aggrieved that you were so noisy when I was trying to make an important call,' rather than 'You are so noisy!' 'It seems to me that you haven't considered my feelings when you've done this,' rather than 'You're so inconsiderate!'
Avoid generalizing.	'You never listen to me!' 'You always do this.' 'How many times do I have to ask you?' 'You always ignore me.'
Ask for what you want rather than just complaining.	'I would like you to keep me informed in future of any developments.' 'I would like you to apologize to me.'
Make requests realistic; for example, don't ask for too many changes at once or too great a change at once.	'I want you to instigate a policy change about this matter for the whole school by next week.' 'I want a complete refund on the entire holiday.'

(contd)

Assertive anger script element	Examples
Try to demonstrate the positive consequences of your request.	'This will allow me to feel more valued as a customer.' 'This will ensure that I don't miss out on important messages again.'
Avoid empty threats.	'If you don't do this, I shall be forced to look for employment elsewhere.' 'If you don't apologize right now I shall withdraw my child from this school.'

Myth buster

Many people believe that they should apologize for getting angry. This is not true; you should only apologize for expressing your anger inappropriately.

Charlotte's story

The same thing winds up Charlotte all the time: the way her husband Zac does nothing to help around the house. They both work, but Charlotte is the one expected to do all the washing, cooking, shopping and childcare. She seems to be in a permanent rage, always furious at having to do so much while Zac watches TV or slips out to the pub after work.

The problem is that whenever she tries to tackle Zac and get him to do more, she is in such a state of rage that she is unable to think straight. She realizes that Zac is very good at sidetracking the issues and she finds that, somehow, the issue they end up rowing about is rarely the one they started on. For example, if she starts yelling at him to put his laundry in the wash basket, Zac somehow manoeuvres the topic to all the things that he does do to help around the house – the time when she was ill and he cooked dinner, the time when she was looking after her mother and he did the shopping *and* put the kids to bed, etc. Somehow she never seems to achieve much by her ranting and raving.

One day she decides to try another strategy. She waits for a calm moment when she isn't enraged by Zac, and sits down over supper to explain how she feels. She focuses on two issues she wants him to help with – stacking the dishwasher and the laundry. She tells him how angry it makes her feel to come home from work to find his breakfast things still on the table and his wet towels on the bedroom floor. She refuses to be sidetracked or to be drawn into a general rant about how generally unhelpful he is. The conversation is productive and Zac agrees to change those two things. Charlotte breathes a sigh of relief; it's a start...

Point to remember

Changing your typical anger 'scripts' from passive or aggressive to assertive is not easy; it takes time and practice as you retrain your mind.

An example of a possible assertive anger script is given for the following situation.

Suzy buys some school shoes for her daughter from a well-known shoe shop. She buys them several weeks before the new term but, within four weeks of her daughter wearing them, the stitching on the buckles becomes loose. She takes them back to the shop to get an exchange but the store claims that, since they are over three months old, no refund is possible. Suzy is angry – the shoes were bought three months ago but the school term only started one month ago, so they have only been worn for four weeks.

Assertive anger script for Suzy

Assertive anger script element	The script
Begin (and end) on a positive note	I am normally very happy with this store and have never had any reason to bring anything back before.
Define the problem specifically and early; don't prevaricate by taking ages to get to the point.	I purchased these shoes in advance because you sell out of girls' school shoes so quickly. The school term started four weeks ago. These are

(contd)

	black school shoes so it is highly unlikely that any child is going to want to wear them out of school. She has thus only worn them for four weeks. They must be faulty.
Use the first person to avoid statements of blame.	I feel that my problem is not being acknowledged here and that I am being accused of lying about my daughter wearing these shoes before starting school.
Explain how you feel.	This makes me feel very angry and disappointed in your reaction.
Don't put yourself down.	I feel I am being penalized for being an organized mum in buying the shoes early.
Focus on the main issue and don't get sidetracked on to past grievances.	The fact that they are also scuffed already is not relevant here – your shoes do scuff within four weeks.
Do criticize the behaviour and not the person.	I don't think you are really listening to me here.
Avoid generalizing.	I am not here to talk about other customers who may or may not have bought these shoes.
Ask for what you want rather than just complaining.	I want these shoes to be replaced or my money back.
Make requests realistic; for example, don't ask for too many changes at once or too great a change at once.	I am not asking for anything more than what is reasonable, even though I have had to make a special trip to town today.
Try to demonstrate the positive consequences of your request.	Replacing these shoes will restore my faith in your store and the value it places in its customers.
Avoid empty threats.	If you don't give me my money back I will never shop at this shoe store again.

Now try writing some suggested assertive anger scripts yourself. Read the following scenario.

A work colleague is annoying you by always trying to get out of doing as much work as possible. She always has an excuse when it comes to taking on an undesirable work project and, consequently, you are angry that you have take on so much of her work. The last straw is that she doesn't do a piece of work she is meant to have done. She waits until she is about to go on annual leave before offloading it gleefully on to you – a day before the deadline.

Create an assertive anger script to tackle her.

Assertive anger script element	The script
Begin (and end) on a positive note.	
Define the problem specifically and early; don't prevaricate by taking ages to get to the point.	
Use the first person to avoid statements of blame.	
Explain how you feel.	
Don't put yourself down.	
Focus on the main issue and don't get sidetracked on to past grievances.	
Do criticize the behaviour and not the person.	
Avoid generalizing.	
Ask for what you want rather than just complaining.	
Make requests realistic; for example, don't ask for too many changes at once or too great a change at once.	
Try to demonstrate the positive consequences of your request.	
Avoid empty threats.	

Assertive anger language

While working through your assertive anger scripts, you will need to ensure that your language is neither aggressive nor passive. This includes both your verbal and your non-verbal or 'body' language. A great deal of communication takes place at the non-verbal level and this often happens subliminally or subconsciously. We may often not be aware of our own body language and the message that we might be sending out; it is especially important to ensure that, if adopting the assertive anger scripts as detailed above, they are not presented with conflicting body language. If your verbal language says one thing (e.g. assertion) and your body language another (e.g. aggression), it is likely that your overall message will be that of aggression, since the non-verbal level of communication is usually more powerful.

> **Quick fix**
> The language you use has a huge impact on whether you express your anger aggressively, passively or assertively.

Some general points to be aware of in terms of assertive body language include the following.

▶ Direct face-to-face stances are seen as more aggressive; try to maintain a slight angle without actually turning away from the other person.
▶ People feel threatened if their personal space is invaded, so keep your distance. A good rule of thumb is that if you can smell or feel the other person's breath, you are definitely too close!
▶ Try to keep your hands still; some hand movements (e.g. fist clenching) can be viewed as signs of aggression, while others (e.g. putting one arm across the chest to clutch at the other arm) are seen as passive.
▶ Your face should match your emotion and what you are saying. Don't laugh when you are upset and don't frown when you are happy. Sometimes people can laugh or smile through nerves when they are angry but this belittles your message.

When you are making an assertive expression of your anger, you need to be heard. In order to be heard you have to pay attention to the tone, the inflection and volume of your voice.

TIPS FOR ASSERTIVE LANGUAGE

▶ Don't forget to listen to the other person and give them the chance to respond.

When we are angry, it is easy to be so caught up in our own feelings that we don't or won't listen to the responses. Listening shows that you are acknowledging and respecting the other person's rights too.

▶ Don't pose statements as questions.

Many of us turn what would otherwise be a simple statement into a question just by letting our voice rise up at the end of the sentence. This is known technically as a high-rising terminal (or HRT) in linguistics, and can be perceived as reflecting uncertainty and nervousness. It's something people's voices do when they are unsure of themselves and seeking approval – although nowadays, it is becoming a more and more popular intonation all the time. Conversely, a falling intonation – where the pitch of your voice drops towards the end of the sentence – is much more assertive.

▶ Don't apologize unless you're actually sorry.

It seems like such a little thing, but the words we choose say much more about us than we might first think. How often do you say 'Sorry' when you don't actually mean it? Do you say sorry when you really mean 'Excuse me' or 'No'? If so, start saying what you actually mean! Saying sorry is essentially a way of accepting blame for something – it sets you up to be submissive. People also apologize for disagreeing or even for being angry, so try to avoid doing this as, again, it diminishes the power of your message.

▶ Let your statements stand on their own.

Avoid those 'add ons' to your sentences that weaken your message because it looks as though you are seeking approval (which is very non-assertive). Examples of unnecessary add-ons include, '...don't you think?', '...do you know what I mean?', 'Know what I'm saying?' and '...if you get my drift'.

▶ Avoid disclaimers.

These are the things we say in order to make us somehow sound humble but that promptly discredit our message. Examples are 'It's just my opinion', or 'You might not agree with me, but...'

There are a lot of things to think about when it comes to expressing your anger using appropriate, assertive language; it takes time and practice to assimilate all the information so keep practising and keep rereading the material.

Other specific aspects of anger language, both verbal and non-verbal, are shown in the following table.

Anger expression	Verbal language	Body language
Aggressive	• Speaks too loudly/ shouts • Uses insults or personalize the issues • May swear Constantly interrupts • Lays blame easily • Uses degrading language	• Waves fists • Points with finger • Has hands on hips • Bangs fists on table • Jabs at other person with finger • Glares • Leans head forward • Leans upper body forward • May invade personal space (gets too close to the other person)
Passive	• Speaks too quietly • Adopts an apologetic tone • Hesitant voice	• Avoids eye contact • Adopts a stooped posture • Bows head • Has 'closed' posture, e.g. arms folded across chest and/or legs crossed
Assertive	• Speaks clearly • Speaks audibly • May repeat requests	• Maintains direct eye contact • Maintains an upright posture • Has 'open' posture, e.g. arms by sides and legs uncrossed • Keeps distance so as to respect personal space

Watching TV

Start becoming aware of the difference between assertive, passive and aggressive language by watching for angry incidents on television. Soaps are usually rife with angry people so, the next time you watch TV, keep a notepad and pen handy. Make a note of the aggressive or passive body language or speech you observe; this will help you become more aware of your own verbal and non-verbal language when you get angry.

Anger expression

The following scenario could have three different responses: aggressive, passive or assertive. Circle all the instances of inappropriate anger expression in the examples below, i.e. when anger is expressed aggressively or passively. The first one in each example is done for you. Then write your own assertive response to the same situation.

Jason is waiting for a space in his local supermarket car park. He has his family with him for the weekly shop, including his toddler in her car seat. He wants to park in a parent-and-child space but none is available, so he waits for a young mum to load up her car and free up a space. He waits patiently, reverses to give her plenty of room to back out, but before he can drive in, another car zooms up and nips into the space. As if this wasn't bad enough, James suspects that this car does not have any small children in it. Indeed he is right: a lone young man leaps out and starts making towards the store.

Aggressive response

Hopping mad, James abandons his car and leaves his wife with the kids while he storms after the driver. He catches up with him and grabs his arm. As the man turns round, James starts shouting loudly, complaining that he has taken a parking space that he had been queuing for and that was for parents with children. The other man reacts immediately and pushes James to stop him gripping his arm. James swears and retaliates by putting his face very close to the man and jabbing his finger close to his eyes, all the time swearing loudly.

The man gets even more aggressive and starts swearing back, pushing him off. James calls him all the names under the sun and looks as if he is going to hit the man.

Passive response

Hopping mad, James abandons his car and leaves his wife with the kids while he storms after the driver. He catches up with him and coughs to get his attention. The man appears not to hear so James mutters 'Er, excuse me?' Again, the man appears not to hear so James tries again, saying 'Excuse me, Sir?' in a louder voice. The man turns round and snarls 'Yes?' at James, which gets James all flustered. Backing away a bit, he glances sideways and tells the man, 'I'm really sorry, but you have taken my parking space. And you've parked in a parent-and-child place and you haven't got a child?' The man glares at James, asks him what he's going to do about it, and stalks away. James is left fuming.

Assertive response

Your turn: can you write a more assertive way for James to express his feelings this time?

Hopping mad, James abandons his car and leaves his wife with the kids while he storms after the driver. He catches up with him and...

Point to remember

Don't be discouraged if you find yourself slipping into your typical anger scripts; retraining your mind out of old habits is a lengthy process and setbacks are a normal part of this.

MOVING ON

This chapter has begun to look at some practical ways of managing anger. We have examined the issue of how we know when it is appropriate to get angry and also at techniques to express anger more appropriately. By examining the ways that people express their anger, you have learned how to swap negative and inappropriate ways of expression for more appropriate and assertive ways.

Key points

1 Recognizing when you have the right to be angry and when you don't is a tricky but important part of the anger management process.

2 If you are to express your anger appropriately, it is essential to recognize the rights of other people while you are feeling and expressing your anger.

3 If you are unsure of your rights and lack confidence in your ability to express anger appropriately, you might adopt a passive style, which can mean you are taken advantage of and left feeling resentful and hostile.

4 On the other hand, being over-confident of your rights and unaware of other people's can mean you come across as too aggressive in your anger expression.

5 Learning to express anger assertively is about paying attention to language and body language (non-verbal communication) as well as the content (script) of your message.

5

Cognitive and behavioural approaches to anger management

How do you feel?
Answer 'true' or false' to the following statements.

- *It's easy to avoid things that make me angry.*   T/F
- *I find it easy to distance myself from what is provoking me.*   T/F
- *I find it easy to empathize with someone who makes me angry.*   T/F
- *I find it easy to distract myself when I get angry.*   T/F
- *I find it easy to do something to make myself feel good when I am angry.*   T/F

The more 'false' answers you gave the more you will benefit from the material in this chapter, which aims to help you find the above coping mechanisms easier to adopt.

Controlling your anger

'*Do not teach your children never to be angry; teach them how to be angry.*'

Lyman Abbott

What happens if it is not appropriate to get angry – but you still feel furious? This chapter considers ways to help you simmer down when you are either getting too angry about a particular situation (and expressing excessive anger) or angry when it is not appropriate to do so (such as when someone won't do what you want). As mentioned repeatedly throughout this book, anger management is not about learning to suppress anger or to try to stop feeling angry; it is about getting angry when it is appropriate to do so and expressing that anger in an appropriate manner.

Cognitive and behavioural approaches to anger management involve both the mental processes (our thoughts) and behavioural processes (what we do). We have already discussed in chapter 3 some of these approaches in relation to the 'angry personality' but here we will look at some specific cognitive and behavioural techniques aimed at controlling our anger when we know we need to cool it – but just can't.

These techniques include:

▶ avoiding the provocation
▶ distancing yourself from the provocation
▶ disrupting your anger response
▶ taking physical exercise.

> **Point to remember**
>
> Anger management techniques can involve changing our mental processing, our actual behaviour, or both.

Avoiding the provocation

Previously (in chapters 2 and 3), we have discussed the avoidance response in reference to a strategy that contributes to the angry personality, so it is important here to distinguish between avoidance as a maladaptive (i.e. negative) anger management strategy (as discussed in chapters 2 and 3) and avoidance as an adaptive (or positive) strategy, as we will see here. The maladaptive avoidance is when the individual avoids dealing with anger – or withdraws from the situation – whereas the strategy to be discussed here is when the individual avoids (or minimizes their exposure to) the provocation or the anger-eliciting event. Avoiding dealing with the anger arousal can be negative and contribute to the angry personality as explained previously, but avoiding the anger-eliciting event can be a positive and helpful strategy.

In chapter 1 we started to chart those 'anger triggers' that cause anger – and to put them into common themes. You will probably notice a recurrence of the sorts of things that make you angry. For many of us, there is a pattern to the things that typically make us angry. For example, a poll carried out by the TV Channel GOLD to mark the 30th anniversary of the hit sitcom *Fawlty Towers* (which features the ultimate in angry characters, Basil Fawlty), shows that Brits lose their rag on average four times a day – more than the Italians or the French. What makes them angry is shown in the graph below.

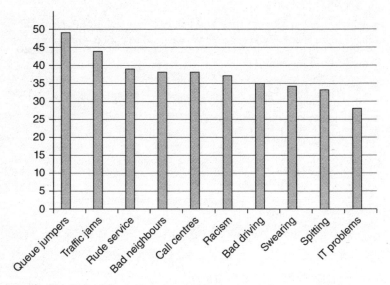

What makes the British people angry (GOLD survey results reported in the Daily Mirror, *15 May 2009)*

A report in the *Daily Mail* (28 April 2012) suggests that the whole nation is getting angrier, with Britons tending to fly into a rage around four times every day. The report suggests that 10 per cent of people claim to have been in an accident caused by road rage.

The article in the *Daily Mail* points out that 'there is anger everywhere, from millionaire footballers screaming obscenities into TV cameras to ordinary people spitting bile at bankers, inflation and greedy MPs'. UK prisons, claims the article, are full of angry people unable to solve problems without resorting to violence. The article cites the case of a woman in Cardiff who launched a physical attack on her local bakery simply because they had sold out of her favourite cupcakes. The Mental Health Foundation estimates that the annual cost to the NHS of all this anger is £105 billion.

How then, can we avoid the things that make us angry? How can we avoid the queue jumpers, the traffic jams and the IT problems? The trick to this technique is to use it sparingly (remember that it is only one tool in the toolbox of skills being developed in this book). Start identifying those anger triggers that can be avoided and those that can't. Go back to the anger diaries from chapter 2 and pick out your common anger triggers to put into the table below. Add more – and keep adding until you have noted most of your triggers (do this over the course of a few weeks to get the best from this exercise). Then go through the triggers and start identifying those that can be avoided and those that can't – with a little note to explain how they can be avoided (if they can). The example below shows you how this anger trigger avoidance plan can be created, using the triggers identified in the GOLD survey as examples.

Anger trigger avoidance plan

Anger trigger	Can it be avoided?	How can it be avoided? If it can't, why can't it?
Queue jumpers	?	I will be more assertive if people cut in front of me in supermarkets. But I can't control what other people do.
Traffic jams on commute to work and home again	✓	By going to work earlier and coming home earlier where possible. I can do this two or three times a week if my partner takes the children to school on those days.
Rude service	✓	Hard to avoid, as I can't control how other people act. However, I can avoid those places where I have had bad service before or where I expect bad service – this includes avoiding people who often make me angry.

(contd)

Anger trigger	Can it be avoided?	How can it be avoided? If it can't, why can't it?
Bad neighbours	✓	If I know I have rude neighbours I can avoid contact with them to a large extent.
Call centres	✗	Call centres are everywhere – hard to avoid them. But try to pick companies that don't use them, or use the internet more rather than ringing.
Racism	✗	I can avoid hanging out with racist or bigoted people but this may be something that I ought to get angry about and not avoid.
Other people's bad driving	✓	Most bad driving is at busy times or when other people are stressed; by travelling outside rush hours I can avoid this to some extent.
Other people swearing	✗	I can't control how other people behave, so hard to avoid.
People spitting	✗	I can't control how other people behave, so hard to avoid.
IT problems	✗	IT problems are probably a fact of everyday life but hard to avoid. I can try to become more IT-savvy by attending training.

Quick fix

Identify the things that typically make you angry and work out which of these triggers can be avoided – and which can't. By avoiding those that can be avoided, you can at least reduce the frequency of anger triggers in your life.

As the above table shows, some anger triggers can be avoided at least some of the time – which leaves fewer to have to tackle with other strategies. Now, make a table of your own, using the same headings as in the table, and develop your own anger trigger avoidance plan, listing the triggers most likely to make you angry.

Myth buster

Most people believe they can't do anything about the things that make them angry but this is not true – some triggers can be reduced or even eliminated.

Distancing yourself from the provocation

It is not always possible to avoid the anger triggers, but it may be possible to distance yourself from them, either physically or temporally. Physical distancing techniques include walking away or moving further away (for example from someone who is being rude or disrespectful to you), going for a walk to cool down or taking some other physical 'time out'. Temporally distancing yourself is just about using time rather than space as a barrier between the anger-eliciting event and yourself; for example, you might ask for time to think over an issue to avoid saying something in anger that you might later regret. This is a useful technique if you are not sure of your rights in the situation or want time to prepare an assertive response (by reading chapter 4, perhaps!).

Quick fix

Sometimes it is possible to distance yourself from anger-inducing triggers by either removing yourself from them or by delaying your exposure to the trigger to a later time.

Other examples of these techniques in action include:

▶ asking to be excused from an anger-eliciting meeting or confrontation while you calm down and gather your thoughts
▶ putting a phone caller on hold while you calm down or discuss an appropriate response with a colleague

▶ refusing to be drawn into a discussion when you know you are angry but requesting a chance to meet up again later to discuss further

▶ asking for a less confrontational way of discussing a problem, such as using email rather than talking face to face.

Choosing a distancing strategy

Read the following descriptions of anger events and decide on a suitable physical and temporal distancing strategy for each one.

Event A Zack is dating but his ex-wife, Debbie, is not at all keen on the idea of their son spending time with Zack's girlfriend during access visits. Debbie is becoming very angry over this issue so, to keep the peace, Zack tells her that his girlfriend will not be present when he takes his son out. The problem is that Zack's girlfriend has been accompanying them, and their son has spilled the beans to Debbie. When Zack drops his son back, Debbie lays into him, screaming and shouting about him lying. Zack reacts by shouting and yelling that he is entitled to do what he wants with his son – and ends up getting aggressive and threatening. The outcome of his outburst is that the police are called, his son is in tears and his ex-wife is now talking about getting an injunction.

1 What physical distancing strategy could Zack have adopted?
2 What temporal distancing strategy could Zack have adopted?

Event B Amira is a teacher and does not get on with one of her colleagues, Julia. Julia is always criticizing Amira and trying to show her up or embarrass her in front of the children or the other teachers. One day, they start a row in the staffroom and later on, when they bump into each other in the corridor, Julia makes a snide comment to the children she is with. Amira reacts angrily and they begin to argue in front of the wide-eyed pupils. Amira loses her temper and starts screaming and swearing at Julia and calling her all the names under the sun. The outcome of this outburst is a summons to see the Head and a suspension.

1   What physical distancing strategy could Amira have adopted?
2   What temporal distancing strategy could Amira have adopted?

Now, consider some examples of when you have been so angry in the past that you have lost your cool and acted in a way that you regretted. What physical or temporal distancing strategies could you have adopted just to get yourself some separation from the anger event – and to give yourself the chance to cool down a little and consider your response from a calmer perspective?

Anger event and outcome	Suggested physical distancing strategy?	Suggested temporal distancing strategy?

Like the avoidance strategy, the distancing technique is not always going to be practical. Sometimes, there is no opportunity for regrouping – your response is either now or never. Even if such strategies are technically possible, it is not always likely that you will be of a calm and rational enough mind to be able to take the decision to remove yourself. This is the whole problem with intense anger – it launches the brain beyond rational thought so that logical steps and sensible strategies become beyond our capability. Practising the strategies helps – even the paper planning that the above exercise tried to stimulate – because it gets you into new habits and new ways of reacting until they become automatic. When this happens, you are more likely to move into the new automatic ways of reacting and stop the older, more impulsive ways of responding.

The next strategy, however, is particularly useful for trying to give yourself some breathing room so that you are able to put other strategies into place.

Myth buster
Some people invest too much energy trying to change or eliminate anger triggers that just can't be changed; instead they should concentrate on changing the way they react to such triggers.

Disrupting your anger response

There may well be instances when something makes us really angry but we feel powerless to do anything about it. We cannot just walk away from the trigger, nor is it something that can be dealt with later. We can't avoid the situation, yet our anger is interfering with our ability to handle it in a calm and rational manner. If we cannot avoid the trigger and we cannot moderate it in any way, the only course of action left is within ourselves (cognitive strategies). We can't change the event but we can change the way we react to it.

One way to do this is by changing the way we interpret anger-inducing events (see chapter 4). Another way to reduce the significance of the event for us is by interfering with the anger response.

When something makes us angry, our mental processes engage the anger response. This begins with an appraisal process that will evaluate the trigger to establish whether it is something that has violated our expectations, blocked our attempts at doing something or in any other way is something that we feel should not have occurred. The appraisal process will also involve an estimate of the other person's intent to cause harm or distress and of the degree to which what has happened is justified (fair) or not. Our individual propensity to anger will play a factor in this appraisal, such that someone with a low tolerance for frustration will be more likely to feel that they should not have to put up with the event (see chapter 3).

The appraisal system will then engage the appropriate level of the anger response to kick in. The anger response consists of physiological, emotional and cognitive changes, as discussed in chapter 2. Physiological changes include the release of adrenal hormones; emotional changes include feelings of annoyance, fury and rage; and cognitive changes often involve the sort of cognitive biases discussed in chapter 3.

The aim of disrupting the anger response, then, is to break the anger response chain. This 'self-disruption' can occur at various points along the chain, either by reappraising the event (see chapter 3 and later in this chapter) or by preventing the anger response from kicking in.

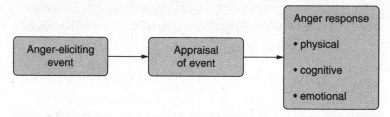

The anger response chain

There are several ways to disrupt the anger response.

1 ENGAGE IN 'INCOMPATIBLE BEHAVIOUR'

Anger is a state of arousal; it is impossible to experience this arousal if you are relaxed. It follows that if you are able to engage in an activity that makes you feel relaxed, it will not be easy for you to feel anger. One way to achieve a general state of increased relaxation is by learning the skill of **deep muscle relaxation** (see chapter 6). Knowing how to physically relax your muscles can lead to a more relaxed state of mind. By performing relaxation exercises, even short forms of them, you are engaging in behaviour that is incompatible with the anger response. The next chapter outlines some more specific relaxation techniques that you can use in response to an angry stimulus or event.

Quick fix

Reduce feelings of anger by breaking the anger cycle; one effective way to do this is by engaging in behaviour that is not compatible with being angry at the same time.

Other things you could try to reduce or limit the anger response include **sporting activities** such as swimming or team games that you enjoy, **creative or artistic pursuits, looking after pets** or anything that you generally find relaxing. Of course, not all these activities will be accessible to you during your normal day (or at work), so you would be more likely to be able to use this technique at the end of the day (see also use of humour in the next chapter).

Interestingly, studies conducted as early as 1977 suggested that other responses that are incompatible with anger (and especially aggression) are **empathy** for the other person and **mild sexual interest** (Baron, 1977). Many of these are concerned with thought processes; this cognitive element will be a focus of the anger-management techniques offered in this chapter and the next. The stimulation of sexual interest, in the other person or in any random person, might be an effective strategy in as much as sexual interest is normally incompatible with anger; however, great care should be taken that such strategies do not lead to inappropriate actions or comments.

Stimulation of empathy for the other person is, however, a more effective 'incompatible' reaction, a fact that led one researcher to describe compassion as the 'psychiatric novocaine' (Stosny, 1995); novocaine is an anaesthetic drug so the implication here is that compassion can anaesthetize you against anger. Inducing compassion and empathy can be achieved through a range of strategies, such as:

▶ imagining that the anger-inducing person is going through a difficult time themselves, with sick family members, redundancy, etc.
▶ learning to put yourself in the other person's shoes until it becomes a habit
▶ searching to find something you might have in common with the anger-inducing person.

Point to remember

If you can conjure up empathy for the person who is making you angry, you will find your anger simmering down somewhat. This can be a helpful strategy if you are worried about your anger getting out of control.

Any positive experience tends to be incompatible with anger – even when that pleasant experience is quite unrelated to the anger event. This is why 'feeling better' in general about life can help us cope better with anger, as the positive response of 'feeling better' is incompatible with feeling angry. Thus, finding ways to induce compassion, empathy or just general positive affect (feeling), will disrupt the anger response. A simple way to do this is to engage in so-called 'pro-social' behaviour when you feel angry: doing something good or altruistic. Engaging in this sort of action makes us feel good about ourselves – a feeling that is often incompatible with the anger response.

Myth buster

When we are angry, it is assumed that we cannot feel positive at the same time. By forcing ourselves to do something good or nice for someone else, we can induce positive feeling – and, yes, this is incompatible with anger so it has the result of reducing the strength of our anger.

Annabelle's story

Annabelle is mum to Jack who often gets into trouble at school. After a few years of this, Annabelle decides to have Jack assessed to see if there is a reason for his difficult behaviour. As part of the assessment process, she needs access to all his school records, which is when she discovers, to her shock, that not only was Jack assessed by a 'diversity and inclusion officer' two years earlier (without her knowledge) but that this assessment had recommended that Jack be referred to an educational psychologist to be assessed for attention deficit disorder (ADD). The recommendation was that he should be assessed sooner rather than later before his problems became worse.

Annabelle sets the assessment wheels in motion and, a year later, Jack is diagnosed with ADD and dyspraxia. However, she receives no proper apology from the school for their failure to pass on this important information about Jack two years ago. They apologize verbally but try to pass the blame, claiming that the inclusion officer told them merely to keep an eye on Jack and only refer if things got worse. Annabelle is angry but feels she can't get anywhere. The school claims that Jack was still placed on the special needs register and had access to support even prior to the diagnosis, so his lack of diagnosis did not make much difference – i.e. he suffered no ill effects from the slower diagnosis. They claim that they don't want to be too quick to label children.

Annabelle feels that there is little she can do but she still feels angry. She just can't let go of the anger, so she decides that the time has come to try to disrupt her anger response. She tries a number of techniques and finds that the most effective ones are 'empathy' (she tries to understand how hard it must be for the Special Educational Needs Co-ordinator at school and that she acted in the best interests of her child) and 'positive mood' (whenever she feels angry she tries to do something to make herself feel good – like meet friends for a lovely hot chocolate at a local café). She also decides to turn her experience into something that can help others by joining a local ADD support group and sharing her experiences so that other parents will know to ask for access to their child's school records early on. Feeling that she is helping others makes her feel a bit less angry.

Try incompatible behaviour strategies

Consider the following list of possible behaviours incompatible with the anger response. Look for opportunities to try out each of the options. When you are next angry, pick an 'incompatible behaviour' from the list and try it; write down the outcome – e.g. whether it was effective. This will help you discover which strategies work best for you so you can adopt them for future use.

Incompatible behaviour	What incident it was used for and the outcome
Relaxation	
Exercise	
Sport	
Humour (e.g. funny film, laugh with friends)	
Inducing empathy	
Pro-social behaviour (doing something nice for someone)	
Inducing positive affect (doing something to feel good, e.g. bubble-filled bath, nice meal)	

2 DO SOMETHING DISTRACTING

This is a technique aimed at distracting yourself from the anger stimulus and thus reducing the intensity of the anger response. When an event causes us to be angry for the first time, we find that we generally never feel as angry as we do that first time the event happened. Our anger fades, not just with time, but also with repeated exposure to the stimulus. This is because our bodies are not capable of maintaining the same level of intense arousal for a long time. This is the case with any intense arousal, which is why the second ride on a roller coaster is never as scary as the first, and why an exciting event is never as exciting when repeated. So, if we can distract ourselves from thinking about the anger stimulus, when we think about it again it should not have quite the same hold on us.

> **Point to remember**
>
> Distraction techniques can work because they disrupt the anger response long enough for us to put things in perspective.

Distraction techniques include both physical and mental techniques. Physical distractions include doing some physical activity that occupies your mind. It does not necessarily have to be a relaxing activity, and you could turn your attention to a particular piece of work that requires your concentration, read an interesting newspaper article or go and talk to somebody about something completely different.

Alexis's story

A colleague tells Alexis that another colleague, John, has made a disparaging comment about Alexis. This makes Alexis fume; she is so angry that she can't think straight. She wants to have it out with John but he is in a meeting. After pacing the floor in her office for a while, she realizes that she can't get anything done – this thing with John is taking over. She can't concentrate on anything but she can't resolve anything either, as John is unavailable.

Alexis decides that she needs to distract herself. Maybe going for a walk will help. She goes for a ten-minute walk in her break and, although this does help focus her mind, it is only focusing her mind on the problem and actually stoking her anger. She returns from her walk and finds John still in his meeting. She decides to find another way of coping with her mounting anger. This time she tries to distract herself by completing her expense forms, a task she always puts off because it is time-consuming and requires concentration – even though it results in money for her.

She forces herself to work through her expenses, concentrating hard to stop herself thinking about John. Knowing that if she doesn't concentrate she might make a mistake and not get her money helps keep her focused. When she has finished she finds that her anger towards John is more manageable and when he finally emerges from his meeting, she is able to confront him in an assertive rather than aggressive way.

Mental distraction techniques include things such as planning a menu for a dinner party or working out a route to a meeting in another part of town. You may not be physically engaged in the distracting activity, but as long as your mind is distracted the technique can work. An advantage of mental distraction is that it is something that can be done 'here and now' without the need to change your situation – very handy if you are at work.

3 USE 'THOUGHT-STOPPING'

This is another cognitive or mental technique that involves you 'catching' the anger response processes and interrupting them. When you feel your anger rising, you interrupt the anger response by telling yourself to 'stop' the thoughts from going around your head. When we are angry, we tend to go over and over in our heads what has happened, which causes the anger cues to be continually reinforced.

Thought-stopping as a technique is especially effective in situations when there is little we can do about the anger event; in other words, nothing productive can come about by continually going over in our mind what has happened.

Since the anger response is not benefiting anyone, it needs to be stopped and you can learn to do this by adopting a 'stop' word or sign that is meaningful for you. This might be saying the word 'stop', 'enough' or 'no' to yourself. It could be visualizing a traffic stop sign. It could even be a physical sign such as pinching your hand or snapping a rubber band on to your hand. Such signs can be enough to stop the stimulus and interrupt the anger response.

Thought-stopping requires practice to make it work for you; people often feel that it doesn't seem to work initially. However, with practice, you can become quite proficient at thought-stopping so it is certainly worth trying. Sometimes you might need to use more directive self-commands, such as:

▶ 'Don't go there!'
▶ 'It's not worth it.'
▶ 'My health is more important than this.'
▶ 'Don't let this get to you.'

There is more on thought-stopping in the next chapter.

Taking physical exercise

Many people report that physical exercise is a useful anger management technique and, indeed, several research studies provide evidence to back these anecdotal reports. For example, an intervention study of hostile adolescents suggested a possible benefit of vigorous exercise (Norris et al., 1992), while others have reported a relationship of anger with physical fitness level, for example a significant correlation between higher levels of aerobic fitness and desirable scores on an anger survey in adults (Stewart et al., 2003). A more recent study (Tkacz et al., 2008) showed that exercise programmes may reduce or prevent an increase in anger expression in children.

There are a number of possible reasons for these findings. Anger is associated with increased prefrontal lobe activity. The prefrontal cortex is the locus of 'executive function', concerning inhibition and self-control. Exercise training has been shown to improve executive function; improvement in executive functioning due to exercise may therefore explain these findings.

••
Quick fix
Engaging in physical exercise when you are angry can significantly reduce the strength and impact of your anger.
••

Another benefit of exercise could be linked with the serotonin theory. Serotonin is thought to increase with exercise but decrease with aggression; it could be that, by increasing serotonin production in the brain, exercise lowers propensity to anger.

Another possible explanation is the misattribution of arousal. When we experience any state of arousal such as anxiety, anger or fear, it is argued that the same feeling underlies any arousal state and it is only our interpretation of that feeling that allows us to label the arousal as 'anger' or 'fear' (see the Wobbly Bridge Study below). If we are exercising, we also experience arousal, which we label as that caused by strenuous activity. If we exercise when we are angry, we might lose the 'anger' label and replace it with a physical arousal label.

The Wobbly Bridge Study

CASE STUDY

In 1974 the psychologists Dutton and Aron visited the Capilano Canyon in Canada, which is crossed by a number of bridges. One bridge is a rickety and apparently unstable suspension bridge 70 m (230 ft) above the canyon that tends to sway, tilt and wobble; users get the impression that they are likely to fall off it into the canyon below. Another bridge is a solid wooden one upstream, and only 3 m (10 ft) above a shallow part of the canyon below. People walking across the rickety bridge tend to be quite aroused with fear – their pulse rate quickens, their heart pounds and they may sweat. Indeed, this may be why they choose that bridge. No such arousal is likely on the lower, solid bridge.

The experimenters interviewed men crossing each of the two bridges and tested how attracted they were to a female confederate on the other side of the canyon. What they found was that the men on the rickety suspension bridge were more attracted to the woman than those on the sturdy bridge. The reason given by the psychologists was that the men on the scarier bridge experience a state of arousal, which, in the presence of a woman, they interpret as attraction to her. The men on the sturdy bridge have no such physical feelings to misinterpret.

This study shows why colleagues at work who have been through some emotional experience together (such as beating a tight deadline or winning a big contract) can end up in a romance – they misinterpret the emotions they are feeling as love!

A further explanation is that strenuous exercise tires us out, which removes the arousal. It is hard to be very tired and yet also extremely angry and that is why we may hear people say, 'I am too tired to care.' Of course, another possibility is that exercise performs a distraction role, since our minds are focused on the physical tasks in hand, and thus complex thought is hindered.

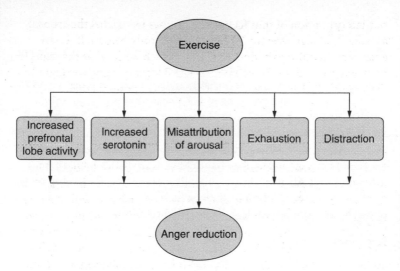

The effects of exercise on anger

MOVING ON

This chapter has looked at some relatively simple anger management strategies that involve avoiding triggers for our anger, distancing ourselves from the source of our anger, disrupting the anger response within ourselves, and engaging in behaviour that is incompatible with the anger response. More of these techniques – such as self-talk and the use of humour – will be discussed in chapter 6, where we will also consider more advanced strategies for anger management such as relaxation techniques and channelling. Knowledge of all these different strategies means that you will soon be able to develop your own personalized toolbox of skills, which will allow you to draw upon the appropriate tools to deal with different situations.

Key points

1 Where possible, a good first step is to try to avoid the anger triggers that you encounter frequently in your life.

2 When this is not possible, the next step would be to try to create some distance, physically or temporally, between yourself and the source of your anger.

3 If you are not able to change the actual anger trigger itself, then you need to move to more cognitive methods and look for ways to disrupt the anger response at some point within the anger cycle.

4 Engaging in behaviour or thoughts that are incompatible with the anger response is an effective way to disrupt the anger response.

5 Using empathy, pro-social behaviour and distraction techniques and taking physical exercise are all effective ways of achieving control of your anger responses.

6

More advanced techniques of anger management

How do you feel?
Answer 'true' or false' to the following statements.

- *When I am angry I am good at talking to myself to help me calm down.   T/F*
- *I am generally quite a relaxed person.   T/F*
- *I am good at finding the humour in most situations.   T/F*
- *I try to find ways to make anger into a force for good.   T/F*
- *I sometimes write letters to people who make me angry – but don't send them.   T/F*

Mainly 'true answers' suggest that you have a good predisposition towards the anger management techniques covered in this chapter, but don't worry if you answered 'false' to some of them – read on to find out how to make these more advanced techniques work for you.

Building on your anger management skills

The basic techniques already covered will often be enough to keep the red mist from descending, or at least from taking over. Sometimes, however, more advanced techniques are needed and this chapter will build on the skills you have developed and enhance your toolbox of skills so that you can manage your anger in any situation.

Techniques covered in this chapter include:

- ▶ using self-talk statements
- ▶ relaxation training
- ▶ desensitization
- ▶ using humour

▶ psychotherapeutic techniques such as the 'empty chair'
▶ channelling anger.

Using self-talk statements

'Consider how much more you often suffer from your anger and grief, than from those very things for which you are angry and grieved.'

Marcus Antonius

Sometimes anger-eliciting events happen that cannot be avoided or for which the strategies outlined in chapter 5 are not appropriate or effective. The use of self-talk statements is a cognitive strategy aimed at either (1) increasing tolerance of the anger-eliciting event, (2) reducing the effect that the event has, or in (3) mobilizing other coping strategies. Self-talk statements are simply the things we can say to ourselves to help put events into perspective. Examples of commonly used self-talk statements come in three categories, and include:

1 increasing tolerance of the anger-eliciting event:
   a 'Worse things can happen.'
   b 'My anger will pass.'
   c 'People say things they don't mean when they are angry.'
   d 'I have to expect these kinds of things to happen.'
2 reducing the effect that the event has:
   a 'If I put this event into the context of my life, it is not worth getting upset about.'
   b 'Will I even remember this event in five years' time, or even in one year's time?'
   c 'My health is more important than this, so I am not going to let it get to me.'
   d 'I am not going to give this person the satisfaction of upsetting me – they are not worth it.'
   e 'In the grand scheme of things, this is not worth getting upset about.'
3 mobilizing other coping strategies:
   a 'I don't have to let this bother me – I can choose how to react.'
   b 'There's no point in reacting while I'm angry – people aren't rational in this state and I might say or do something I'll regret.'
   c 'Letting this go is not a sign of weakness.'

We can learn to reduce the impact that an anger-inducing event
has on us and so reduce the intensity of the anger that we feel.

It is useful to study the statements above, add your own personal
ones (for example, 'I have just had heart surgery – this event
is not important compared to that.') and pick out those you
find most helpful. It can be useful to write down your self-talk
statements under the three categories shown above and to collect
a list that works for you. Then, internalize them by making them
part of your everyday cognitive processes. Practise saying them
and believing them before an anger-eliciting event happens. You
could use visual imagery, too, if appropriate, such as imagining
your blood bubbling away as your blood pressure rises. By
internalizing the statements, you will be ready to draw on them
when you need them.

Quick fix

Making a collection of self-talk statements that work for you in terms of
helping you put things into perspective can be a valuable addition to your
toolbox of skills.

Using self-talk

What self-talk statements could be used in the following scenario?

Sara is due on a work assignment one evening and needs her
husband, Chris, to be back in time to take care of the children.
Sara has to leave the house at 6 p.m. and Chris promises to be back
in good time. Unfortunately, Chris is not known for his punctuality
or reliability and so Sara texts him a couple of times during the
day to remind him – and to point out how important it is that he
isn't late. Of course, the inevitable happens and he doesn't get back
until 6.15 p.m. Chris trots out the usual excuses about the traffic
and so on, but Sara is livid – really blazing angry. As she sets off
in a huff, she realizes that she needs to get a grip and calm down
before her meeting.

What self-talk strategies would help Sara in the three categories?

1 increasing tolerance of the anger-eliciting event
2 reducing the effect that the event has
3 mobilizing other coping strategies

Possible answers (don't read these until you have written your own):

1 increasing tolerance of the anger-eliciting event:
    a 'Chris is unreliable but he did not purposely want me to
      be late.'
    b 'I should expect Chris to be late – that is normal for him.
      I should always give him a time well in advance of when
      I really need him.'
2 reducing the effect that the event has:
    a 'So, I will be a few minutes late myself – it is frustrating but
      the client is not going to be bothered, especially as I can
      ring them.'
    b 'This won't affect my life.'
3 mobilizing other coping strategies:
    a 'I'm angry at Chris's thoughtlessness, not because he
      was late *per se*. If I can accept that he did not do this
      maliciously, I can let go of my anger.'
    b 'I'm not going to get raised blood pressure over this and
      risk my health – nor am I going to allow this to cloud my
      attitude to my client by being angry.'

Relaxation training

As we have seen, relaxation is a state incompatible with anger.
Many researchers have shown relaxation to be an effective way to
manage anger (e.g. McKay and Rogers, 2000), and it is useful to learn
some specific techniques aimed at inducing a relaxed state that is
incompatible with the anger response. Progressive (or deep) muscle
relaxation is a technique that, practised regularly, can help you
become more relaxed in general. This should help keep your arousal
levels lower so that it will take more provocation to make you angry.

This technique then, is aimed at reducing general levels of tension
rather than episodic states of tension that occur in response to a
specific event or episode. It can be adapted to a shortened version that

you can use in response to anger-eliciting events (see below), but you can train yourself in other relaxation techniques so that you will be:

▶ able to reduce your levels of anger and arousal in response to an anger-eliciting event
▶ less likely to get aroused in the first place.

All relaxation techniques make use of the incompatibility of anger arousal with the state of relaxation.

Quick fix
Learning to relax more in general will lower the likelihood of you getting angry; while learning quick relaxation techniques to use when you do get angry can help you manage your anger when it does occur.

Progressive muscle relaxation

This technique will help you learn the difference between tension and relaxation in the body. Many relaxation techniques rely on telling people to 'relax' but this is actually quite hard to do. Progressive muscle relaxation works by teaching you to tense each muscle in turn, and then to relax it, so that you can really feel the difference between tension and relaxation. Try it yourself:

1 Sit comfortably in an armchair or you can even lie on a bed. Close your eyes for best effect (but not if it makes you uncomfortable).
2 Concentrate on your breathing – breathe in and out really slowly. Every time you breathe out, say to yourself the word 'relax'. Do this several times.
3 Now start with your toes. Curl and tense your toes tightly until it feels uncomfortable. Notice how tensing your toes makes your calves and even your thighs uncomfortable too. Notice how tensing just your toes can spread the tension through your body.
4 Now, relax your toes and enjoy the feeling of relaxation this produces. Notice the difference between tension in your toes and relaxation. Every time you breathe out, say to yourself the word 'relax'.
5 Repeat.
6 Now move on to your thighs. Tense your thighs tightly until it feels uncomfortable. Notice how tensing your thighs spreads the tension throughout your body, to your stomach and even your arms.

7 Now, relax your thighs and enjoy the feeling of relaxation and warmth that this produces. Notice the difference between tension in your thighs and relaxation. Every time you breathe out, say to yourself the word 'relax.'

8 Repeat.

9 Now move on to your stomach. Tense it tightly until it feels uncomfortable. Notice how tensing your stomach muscles spreads the tension throughout your body.

10 Now, relax your muscles and enjoy the feeling of relaxation and warmth that this produces. Notice the difference between tension in your stomach and relaxation. Every time you breathe out, say to yourself the word 'relax'.

11 Repeat.

12 Repeat this tensing and relaxing of each muscle group in turn: your fingers (clench into tight fists), shoulders (shrug them to your neck), eyes (squeeze them tightly closed) and face (scrunch up your mouth). Finally, tense your whole body and relax it.

You can adapt this technique to use as a quick response when you experience an anger-eliciting event. If something or someone gets you really angry, you are obviously not always (or even often) going to be able to disappear to a quiet place with an easy chair to engage in a full deep muscle relaxation programme. However, there are quick and unobtrusive ways to do a brief version and this works especially well if you are already regularly practising the full version at home.

Point to remember

Learning to do progressive muscle relaxation properly takes time, so give yourself plenty of opportunity to practise – don't wait until you are really angry before trying it out.

The key is to tense and relax the different muscle groups in turn rather than every part of your body at the same time. Start by tensing and relaxing your arms (including fists, biceps and forearms). Next, move to your back and stomach (tensing and relaxing once or twice) before finishing with your legs (including toes and calves). It is useful to use a trigger word such as 'relax' that you may have been using for the full relaxation exercise (see above); if you have been practising the full technique using such a trigger word, then saying it to yourself should act as a kind of Pavlovian trigger to relaxation because you will have subconsciously learned to associate that word with the state of relaxation.

Desensitization

When something has happened that has made you really angry, there are times when there is either nothing you can do about it or you just wish you didn't feel so angry about it. Anger is debilitating and can stop you concentrating on other things. If only you could somehow get that anger to dissipate. Desensitization is a useful technique for such situations: it will enable you to interrupt the anger response by stopping your anger altogether rather than avoiding or dealing with the stimulus.

Desensitization works on the principle that the more you are exposed to a stimulus, the less arousing it will be. This applies to many situations. For example, phobias are often treated with a graded desensitization approach that allows the sufferer gradually to come into more and more contact with the feared stimulus until it stops being arousing. Our bodies are designed to habituate or become accustomed to arousing stimuli – if we let them. What often happens, particularly with phobias, is that as soon as we get aroused, we avoid the stimulus, which does not allow us to build up the resistance.

If you cannot get an angry episode out of your mind and find it keeps interrupting your work, try a desensitization approach. If you couple this with relaxation it will be twice as effective. You will, ideally, need a quiet place to do this, so this is probably a technique best done at the end of an 'angry' day:

How to become desensitized

1 Lie back in an easy chair and close your eyes. Concentrate on your breathing, which should be slow and steady. Every time you breathe out, say to yourself the word 'relax'.
2 Concentrate on your muscles and make sure that they are relaxed, by tensing and relaxing them each in turn.
3 Now, relive the events that made you so angry. Go through in your mind exactly what happened and how you felt. As you do so, keep your breathing nice and slow and keeping saying to yourself the word 'relax' every time you breathe out.
4 As you relive the anger-inducing event, notice how it makes you feel. Keep reliving the event until it no longer makes you feel so angry. This might take some time but it will eventually happen.

Using humour

'A person without a sense of humour is like a wagon without springs. It is jolted by every pebble on the road.'

Henry Ward Beecher

Humour is another cognitive or mental technique that relies on the introduction of something incompatible with the anger response. Just as certain behaviours such as relaxation techniques are incompatible with anger arousal, so is using affect, or feelings, as the incompatible stimulus. The basic premise of using humour is that we cannot feel both angry and amused at the same time. Laughter will thus replace rage.

Humour can also be used to put events into perspective by interrupting the appraisal part of the anger response; when we can laugh at something, we interpret the event differently. This is why people may say to you, 'You'll laugh about this one day' (often when you cannot imagine that day ever coming). Laughing can also interrupt the anger response by providing an emotional release from the tension. Humour can also be used as a distracter – make someone laugh and they might forget why they were angry in the first place.

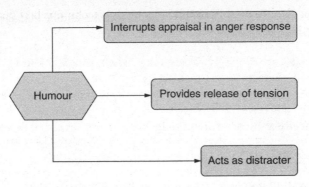

```
┌──────────────────────────────────────────┐
│ Interrupts appraisal in anger response     │
└──────────────────────────────────────────┘

⬡ Humour ──────► ┌──────────────────────────┐
                 │ Provides release of tension │
                 └──────────────────────────┘

                 ┌──────────────────┐
                 │ Acts as distracter │
                 └──────────────────┘
```

The effects of using humour

Using humour in anger-inducing situations is a skill in itself. The humour should not be hostile, sarcastic or directed at someone with malicious intent. Instead, it is about training yourself to find something funny in what has happened or what has been said. Examples of humour that can be found include:

▶ the appearance of the other person in an angry encounter; perhaps their face is red with rage or they look as if they are going to 'explode'

▶ your (or the other person's) angry words coming out wrong or getting something mixed up

▶ your 'opponent' using ludicrous insults or exaggerated putdowns.

THE BENEFITS OF LAUGHTER

The physical effects of humour (in particular laughter) appear similar to those of exercise, with a huge range of benefits ascribed to it over the years: increasing alertness (because of adrenalin, norepinephrine and dopamine secretions), increasing respiration, increasing muscle activity and heart rate, increasing pleasure and decreasing pain (because of endorphin secretion). Laughter has also been shown to be accompanied by changes to IgA, which is an important immune enhancer in our bodies (Moran and Massam, 1997).

You would probably be wise to refrain from laughter while the other person is present, as this can really inflame an already fraught situation (see chapter 7 on conflict). However, once the encounter is over, you can relate the story to colleagues or a partner in a way that emphasizes the humorous aspect; for example, a colleague of mine was once called a 'cow', even though he is male, and he managed to find this amusing rather than insulting.

Of course, care should always be taken when using humour to diffuse angry situations to ensure that it is used judiciously. Successful use of humour can ensure that you avoid many arguments and flare-ups, but there is always the risk that it can make an already tense situation even more explosive – with the anger increasing instead of decreasing.

Point to remember

Use humour carefully as an anger management technique, making sure that you are not using it in a way that will wind the other person up more.

It is probably best not to use humour in response to someone else being angry about a perceived injustice; when a person feels that they have been dealt with unfairly, they are unlikely to be very responsive to finding humour in the emotive situation they are in. Humour might be more successful when dealing with more minor disagreements or when something has escalated from a minor disagreement ('I can't believe we are getting so worked up over a chocolate bar').

Quick fix
Looking for the humour and fun in every incident will help you reduce your propensity to get angry.

Using humour to diffuse anger

Example 1: Steve is arguing fiercely with his wife, Lynne, over who does the most work around the house. Each accuses the other of not doing enough and the anger levels are building, as each side feels hard done by. How could humour be used to prevent the anger escalating?

Possible answers: One or other of them could notice how similar their argument sounds to their kids arguing about whose turn it is to clear the table. They could use this comparison in a humorous way by either mimicking their children (saying childish things such as 'You are such a loser!' or using childish insults like 'Meaneypeg!') or by pointing out the similarity ('Look at us - we are no better than the kids!').

Example 2: Annabelle is angry because she feels that her boss has embarrassed her in a meeting in front of her colleagues. Her boss ridiculed her ideas and made her feel foolish. Annabelle did not feel she could easily retaliate and found her anger boiling over. How could she use humour to cope?

Possible answers: Annabelle could draw a funny caricature of her boss with an oversized nose, warts, claws, etc. (but making sure to destroy the drawing afterwards). She could make up a funny limerick about him, or later on, tell the tale of what he had said but with humorous embellishments ('He looked down his nose at me and spoke in a really snooty voice – he sounded like he was constipated,' etc.).

Michelle and Natasha's story

Michelle's 12-year-old daughter, Natasha, has a medical condition that requires frequent hospital appointments, medication and occasional procedures. This involves time off school for Natasha and juggling of work schedules for Michelle.

Natasha is on a new medication and requires blood tests at the start of the new regime and four weeks later to ensure that her blood electrolytes remain stable. Natasha finds blood tests very difficult and it often takes three or four attempts in different veins to obtain the blood.

When the results of the second test come back to show that Natasha's potassium levels are low, she and Michelle are not too thrilled to learn that yet another blood test will be required. Two weeks later, they duly turn up – Natasha is taken out of school and Michelle takes the afternoon off work – for the test and a consultant appointment after it. The blood test goes OK but, instead of seeing their usual consultant, they are shown to his registrar who doesn't know them. This means another drawn-out history taking with the new medic – which is tiresome for Natasha and her mother.

However, the real problem comes when the registrar expresses surprise that Natasha has just had a blood test because the latest letter about her results shows they are normal. After some confusion, it transpires that the consultant was way behind when looking at the blood results and the abnormal result was for the first blood test, not the second one. Natasha's second test was normal so the third one she has had that day was unnecessary.

Both Michelle and Natasha are furious at the wasted afternoon for them and the unnecessary pain that Natasha had to endure, all because the consultant didn't look at the blood results for four weeks!

Rather than fuming, Michelle and Natasha start to see the humour in the situation and joke to each other about their lazy consultant – imagining that he spent the four weeks watching TV and playing computer games instead of checking Natasha's results. They take the joke further by imagining that he likes to while away his time trying to find ways to annoy his patients; 'I know, I will make them come in for an unnecessary blood test – that will really annoy them!'

Before long, Michelle and Natasha are giggling away and their anger is diffused.

Are you laughter challenged?

Adding humour to your life in general terms can tone down your angry personality and help you find the fun in situations that might otherwise have made you angry. Answer the following questions to see if you need more laughter and fun in your life.

Question	1 Rarely	2 Sometimes	3 Often	4 Frequently
1 How often do you really laugh during a normal day?				
2 How often do you laugh at yourself?				
3 How much do you do things just for fun?				

Question	1 Rarely	2 Sometimes	3 Often	4 Frequently
4 How often do you watch funny films/TV programmes/read funny books?				
5 How often do you get a chance to have a laugh with friends?				
6 How much do you surround yourself with people who make you laugh?				
7 How often do you find something funny in things that happen to you?				

How to interpret your score
A score over 20 indicates plenty of laughter in your life while a lower score suggests you could do with more. See below for ideas for how to bring more laughter and fun into your life.

LAUGHTER YOGA

Laughter yoga is a combination of laughter exercises with yogic breathing (*Pranayama*). It increases the amount of oxygen in your body while you are also being playful, resulting in a feeling of being more healthy, energized and alive. This exercise actually changes the physiology of your body so that you start to feel happier.

> '*Laughter yoga is based on the concept of laughing for no reason except that it is good for us! It is not based on jokes, but rather incorporating into gentle exercise a willingness to laugh, plus yogic breathing. With a sense of playfulness, this soon leads to real laughter.*'

Robin Graham, laughter yoga trainer, Manchester, UK

Using the 'empty chair'

This technique is a psychotherapeutic strategy sometimes used in therapy. It is derived from a school of psychology called gestalt therapy (Perls, Hefferline and Goodman, 1965). Angry clients are asked to imagine that the person who has made them angry is actually sitting in an empty chair opposite them and they are then encouraged to express themselves in the first person to the chair – as if the other person were really sitting there.

A wife who is angry with her husband for having an affair, for example, might say to her 'empty chair': 'I feel so angry that you have betrayed me. You've shown me no respect and you have not given a single thought to my feelings. How dare you treat me this way?'

The idea of the technique is that it helps the client experience and understand their feelings more fully, by helping them identify exactly why they are angry (in the above example, it is because they feel betrayed and disrespected).

To develop this technique further, the client could then take the role of the empty chair and imagine how they might respond to the accusations levelled at them: 'I didn't mean to disrespect you – it was just a stupid fling.'

This helps clarify feelings and reactions as well as possibly allowing the client insight to see things from the other person's perspective.

The empty chair

Think back to a time when someone made you really angry. It could be your partner/spouse, your child, your boss, a customer, a shop assistant or a random stranger on the bus. Imagine that they are sitting on an empty chair in front of you. This is your chance to confront them. You can do this in one of three ways, depending on what you feel most comfortable with.

1 A verbal dialogue

You will need an empty room with no chance of you being observed. This works best if you are confident of not being overheard so that you can shout or scream if necessary.

2 A written dialogue

Many people feel uncomfortable talking to an empty chair (for obvious reasons) or don't have the privacy required. Instead, write down the conversation that you would have with the person in your empty chair.

3 A letter

This is not a dialogue but a one-way communication. Write as much as you can in your letter – but don't send it.

After the exercise, ask yourself the following questions:

- ▶ Do you feel that you have 'let your anger out'?
- ▶ Do you feel that you have understood your feelings better?
- ▶ Do you feel that you have identified exactly what it is that has made you so angry?
- ▶ Do you feel any better?

The exercise should give you an insight into your reactions and feelings so that you can identify exactly what it is about the situation that is making you angry. For example, someone being rude to you might not be the real cause of your anger; what is really making you angry is the fact that you couldn't come up with a suitable retort at the time.

The empty chair technique aims to provide a safe outlet for your feelings, so don't use it if your outburst could be overheard or if you feel silly talking to an empty chair. The insights and self-awareness you gain from using the technique should help you feel better about the situation and dissipate your angry feelings.

Channelling anger

'The world needs anger. The world often continues to allow evil because it isn't angry enough.'

Bede Jarrett

In trying to manage, control and reduce our own anger, it is easy to lose sight of the benefits of anger. As discussed in chapter 1, anger is a valuable motivating emotion and, when channelled appropriately, can have great benefits. Many parents who have lost children to disease, murder victim relatives and victims of other injustices have channelled their anger into campaigns aimed at improving conditions for others or to prevent such things happening again. Anger, when channelled properly, can be the driving force behind positive change for you or others.

Mere acceptance that anger can be a positive force can be enough to reduce arousal levels in a situation. In other words, much of the arousal of an angry event is tied up within the knowledge that you somehow shouldn't be angry, that anger is bad and that you must try to control it. Turning this idea on its head, and acknowledging not just your right to be angry but also the benefits that could accrue, will take away much of the internal tension, and so taking this cognitive view can in itself offer therapeutic benefits.

Channelling anger allows you to turn a negative force into something positive, to right a wrong or bring about change.

Once you have decided to channel your anger there are two potential difficulties. The first is knowing what do with the anger and the second is staying motivated. Since states of arousal cannot be continuously perpetuated, maintaining that arousal long enough to take action can sometimes be problematic.

Angry reaction to obesity campaign

According to a BBC News Online report (9 February 2012), a campaign in America to tackle childhood obesity backfired because of the anger it caused parents of larger children. The campaign, started by a hospital in Georgia, used hard-hitting images of overweight children accompanied by chilling warnings about their future health.

Parents of overweight children reacted angrily to the campaign, however, fearing that it would lead to their children being targeted by bullies or stigmatized. One parent was so angry that she started her own counter-campaign aimed at sending out positive messages about children regardless of their size. On the first day her campaign raised $12,000.

HOW TO CHANNEL YOUR ANGER

When we are very angry it is hard to be rational and objective, but if we are to channel our anger rationality is essential. Channelling anger is about turning what has happened into some kind of positive outcome, either for you as a wronged individual or for the 'greater good' of humankind (or at least the people in your organization). Channelling anger utilizes a problem-solving approach.

A good first step is to write down what has happened – something you may already have done if you are keeping an anger diary (see chapter 1). Here, however, instead of just considering the event and its associated emotions/cognitions, consider what you could do either to prevent the event happening in the first place or to change the outcome of the event. It might be that a different organizational system or more efficient process could make a difference and prevent a recurrence of what happened.

Anger channelling records are a useful way to document these processes. The following example shows you what one might look like and how to complete it.

Anger channelling record

The problem	Alice's work involved some overseas travel. Because she worked for a large institution (a university), there was a lot of paperwork to complete and bureaucracy to go through in order to get payment and expenses authorized. The university had a system of paying for hotel accommodation direct so that the employee did not have to pay out large sums and claim them back. This involved giving the details to the finance department to book the accommodation.
	On one occasion, when about to set off for a conference to St Louis, USA, Alice became concerned that she had no confirmation of her hotel booking. It transpired that the finance department had forgotten to book her hotel. Furious, she contacted the hotel herself but it was fully booked, as were all the hotels in the vicinity. She had to settle for a distant hotel involving taxi rides to and from the conference venue, instead of being on site as planned.
The feeling	She was very angry with her finance department who curtly told her that it was her responsibility to check the arrangements. She was furious that she had to check that they hadn't made mistakes, but decided to channel her anger.
Channelling	She decided that the finance department was 'useless' and she introduced a tagging system so that she could double-check anything that involved them. She extended her personal checking system to other situations and departments and a year on, actually felt that some good had come out of the experience.

An article in the *Basingstoke Gazette* (3 April 2010) reported that a former deputy leader of Basingstoke and Deane Borough Council has called for more 'angry young people' because these are the people who can bring about much-needed change in the area.

The councillor, ahead of his stepping down at the local elections, claimed that it was anger that had drawn him into politics a decade earlier and that it is this anger that can create the passion for change that is still needed today.

Channelling anger towards some positive outcome may involve suggestions for change at various levels and this is likely to involve persistence. Others may be resistant to your ideas for change, particularly in large institutions where things have 'always' been done a particular way. Prepare your case by writing down the proposed scheme and its benefits. Mention your experience but do not get too emotional about it – the idea is to present rational, not emotion-driven, change. If other people have had a similar experience this evidence can be used to add weight to your argument.

MAINTAINING THE MOTIVATION

In trying to channel the anger, you may be lucky and achieve the results you want fairly quickly. If, however, you are taking on a big corporation, you may have to face setbacks. If your initial anger dissipates it is at this point that you are likely to give up. Remember that anger is the motivating force here and, like most strong emotions, it does tend to fade with time. This is especially so if you have talked about the incident a lot with others or relived it in your mind a great deal. Maintaining the motivation to act over a long period of time can become a problem.

There are two ways of looking at the issue. On the one hand, if your motivation has waned it is likely that your anger has dissipated, in which case you could leave it at that. If you are not angry, why persevere? On the other hand, you might still be determined to effect some change and, in these cases, it can be useful to try and maintain or regenerate the anger. This sounds rather strange advice, especially in an anger management book, but it is advice that serves to remind us that anger is not all bad and destructive and that it can be an important motivating source.

Diminished anger can actually be maintained or regenerated by doing some of the same things you did to get rid of it in the first place! Reliving the experience, rereading your anger diaries and talking again to people – these are techniques that can induce the emotion to some extent but only if there has been a time delay since you last engaged in such activities. If a few months have passed since the event and since you talked about it or relived it, then engaging in these behaviours can induce the anger again (although not with the same strength as the initial feeling). The resurgence of anger should keep your motivation to act going a little longer.

MOVING ON

This chapter has examined some of the more advanced techniques of anger management that you can add to your toolbox of anger management tools. The trick is to select the tools that work best for you in a given situation. These techniques are mainly about turning down our own heat; the next chapter looks in more detail about turning down other people's heat during conflict resolution.

Key points

1 Cognitive self-talk strategies can be extremely useful in helping put anger episodes into perspective and to minimize the effect they can have on our emotional health.

2 If we have a generally relaxed and laid-back attitude we will be less likely to get angry in the first place, so learning relaxation skills is of great use.

3 Humour is a valuable tool in our anger-management armoury and it can fulfil a range of functions; remember that it is hard to laugh and be angry at the same time.

4 Some psychotherapeutic techniques such as the 'empty chair' can be useful, although not everyone will be comfortable using them; the idea is to find strategies that work for you and these may vary according to circumstance.

5 Channelling your anger so that something good results from your negative feelings means that your anger has had a purpose.

7

Turning down the heat: conflict resolution

How do you feel?
Answer 'true' or false' to the following statements.

- *When other people get angry with me, I tend to get angry back. T/F*
- *When someone is angry with me, I prefer just to walk away. T/F*
- *Other people's anger tends to make me defensive. T/F*
- *In a conflict situation, it is important for me to prove I am right. T/F*
- *I would never agree with someone or apologize in order to placate them. T/F*

If you answered 'true' to more than two of these questions, it may well be that managing other people's anger is difficult for you. While managing our own anger can be a complex process to learn, involving the accumulation of a range of new skills, coping with other people's anger can seem much harder because of the unpredictability involved. However, if you can develop the capability to de-escalate anger, you will have the basis of a new skillset for resolving a conflict situation.

Why other people get angry

Other people around us get angry for the very same reasons we do! When their anger is directed towards us, we need to understand the range of possible reasons for this anger. These reasons can fall into a number of themes:

▶ They feel let down or betrayed by us.
▶ They feel we have insulted them.

- They believe that we have not met their expectations.
- They believe that we have wronged them/treated them unjustly or unfairly.
- They feel embarrassed.
- They know that they are wrong but get angry to save face.
- They don't feel they are being listened to or understood.
- They feel frustrated.

Working out the causes of anger

Consider the following scenarios and try to work out the real reason why the other person became so angry.

A Jazz was shopping in a no-frills supermarket with his children. When it was time to pay, he headed for the checkouts. On seeing two possible tills with small queues, he suggested that his 12-year-old wait in one line and he would wait in the other and see which one was quicker. In the event, his son's line was quicker and he sped across with his trolley and nipped into the place 'reserved' by his son. The man behind took exception to this and flew into a rage about queue jumping.

Why do you think the other shopper became so angry?

B Jazz then visited a different supermarket. He parked in a parent-and-child bay as usual. As he hopped out with his oldest child, a woman came up to him and started berating him for using a parent-and-child bay. He explained that he was entitled to use it as he did have children, but she complained that his kids were too old to warrant the use of such a bay. Jazz looked behind him and indicated his middle child who was still at the car and helping his youngest daughter, a three-year-old, out of her car seat. The woman changed tack and got angrier – this time complaining that he shouldn't be leaving another child in charge of a three-year-old like that.

Why had the woman become angry at first – and what was the reason for her continued anger?

C Jazz then went home. He unloaded the shopping from the car and left it in the hall. Pretty exhausted at this stage, he made himself a cup of tea and sat down in front of the TV. His youngest sat watching with him and his other two went off to play on the Nintendo Wii. Then his wife came home from work and immediately flew into a rage, complaining about the shopping in the hall, the fact that the older kids weren't doing their homework and the fact that the younger one was watching unsuitable TV.

Why do you think she was angry?

Answers

A The other shopper probably became angry because he felt that his rights had been violated, i.e. he had been wronged. He clearly felt that using your child to reserve a place in the line was unfair.

B Here the other shopper started being angry because she felt that Jazz had done something wrong, unjust or unfair (by taking a space he wasn't entitled to). As it dawned on her that she was wrong and that he was entitled to the space, she probably became embarrassed and unwilling to lose face. This actually fuelled her anger so she changed tack in order to direct it at something more appropriate.

C His wife probably felt let down by Jazz. She had come home from work and her expectations (of an orderly house with children engaged in appropriate activities) were not met from the moment she stepped through the door. She probably felt wronged and frustrated too.

Point to remember

Trying to work out the real reason why someone is angry can pay dividends; the obvious cause of their anger isn't always the real cause.

Dealing with other people's anger: top tips

1 Acknowledge their emotion
The first step to dealing with other people's anger is to acknowledge their emotion; this shows the other person that you understand that

they are angry and why they are angry. Often, people get angrier and angrier simply because they feel the need to make clear just how angry they actually are. Acknowledging that you have recognized how angry they are can take the wind out of their sails and they no longer need to keep showing you the intensity of their feelings (more on this later).

Jenny's story

Jenny has set up a new business selling party products and she registers the business on as many free listing sites as possible. One of these sites is a local business directory, which is when her problems start. She begins to be inundated with phone calls to her mobile, from companies trying to sell her everything from phone packages to electricity, gas, double-glazing and advertising space. Every ten minutes there is another of these calls, and her clients can barely get to speak to her.

Furious, she rings customer services to complain bitterly about her details being sold on for marketing purposes. She fully expects the company to be defensive and to say they were entitled to sell her details on. However, she is taken aback when the customer service operator immediately apologizes and shows real understanding of how frustrating all the calls must be for her. She promises to remove her details immediately from the marketing lists and even says that she will take this issue back to the team to see if they need to make an opt-out clause clearer for people signing up to their directory. She also suggests that Jenny register with the telephone preference service (TPS) to make sure that other companies don't drive her mad.

Jenny feels her anger totally dissipate. Here is someone who understands how she feels and why she was so angry. What a relief!

2 Distance yourself
It is important, while you are acknowledging the anger, not to take the emotion too personally. People say things they don't mean when they are very angry and they might not actually be angry with you personally. If you try to distance yourself a little, you can prevent your own emotions getting involved, which can lead to an escalation

of the anger instead of turning down the heat (as you get angry, which makes them more angry, etc.).

3 Listen well

Try not to jump to an immediate conclusion or to leap to a defence without full consideration of the complaint at hand. If someone is verbally attacking you, it is normal to want to defend yourself, but it can be beneficial to hold back and wait until you have heard the full complaint and thought about the issues involved. Listen carefully (more on this later) before responding – this will also afford the other person the opportunity to vent a bit.

This does not mean that you have to put up with abuse; if the other person is swearing or calling you names, you are fully entitled to ask them to stop doing that. Do this in an assertive but friendly manner, e.g. 'Hey, please don't swear at me', or 'I have to ask you to lower your voice a little.'

4 Lose the audience

If the conflict is developing in a public place, it is a good idea to try to steer the angry person to a more private space. Privacy will help prevent other people from getting involved in the conflict, which can make things far worse and cause a smaller problem to escalate. Moving to a more private area also takes away the audience for the angry person, which can change the way they behave and help them save face if they are to back down later. However, if you feel in any way vulnerable, never go anywhere totally private (see point 7).

5 Keep your voice calm and low

Concentrate on keeping your tone of voice calm and your pitch low. A low voice and calm tone will help to reduce the intensity of the other person's anger. If you were to respond to the other person's shouting by matching their intensity, you will only escalate the strength of the rage rather than diminishing it – this is because the louder you become, the louder they will become to match your level.

6 Ask the person to sit down

Consider getting the angry person to sit down somewhere with you; it is harder to get excessively angry from a seated position. People tend to stand up when they are very angry so trying to keep people seated can counter this automatic response.

7 Seek help or an escape route if in danger

If you feel in any danger or at risk of physical attack, seek help if possible. If this is not possible, seek a quick escape route (e.g. say you have to go), which can provide 'calming down' time.

8 Use self-calming strategies and reflection

After the event, use your own anger-reducing or calming strategies as outlined in previous chapters of this book; good reflection skills will help you deal with what happened and see what skills you used.

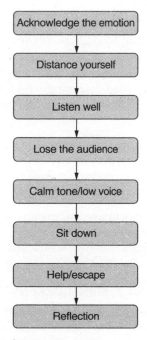

Steps for dealing with another person's anger

Conflict escalation: heating and cooling elements

Conflict is what can result when two parties strongly disagree over something. Conflict does not necessarily involve anger, but almost always does. This is because conflict is more than just a disagreement: it is a situation in which one or both parties perceive a threat (whether or not the threat is real) and this can trigger strong emotions.

> **Myth buster**
> Conflict does not always have to involve anger and can be resolved peacefully. However, conflict often provokes strong emotions, which is why anger is often an integral part of it.

Conflict can escalate easily, especially if certain conditions are met. It is useful at this point to identify the sorts of actions and reactions that can lead to an escalation of angry conflict: the 'heating elements'. Each 'heating element' also has its corresponding 'cooling element' (which can de-escalate the conflict), as outlined below.

HEATING ELEMENT 1: TRYING TO AVOID THE CONFLICT

When someone annoys us, suppression of the feeling can lead to avoidance of conflict – which might seem like a good idea. However, this desire to avoid conflict can just lead to a build-up of pent-up anger, which can then explode in an angrier outpouring than the initial conflict warranted. It is thus much healthier to address conflict sooner rather than later.

Cooling element: Avoid this by trying to deal with conflict when it arises and encouraging others to do the same.

> **Point to remember**
>
> Avoiding conflict by refusing to discuss the issue or by walking away isn't always a good strategy; it can simply lead to a build-up of resentment and an even bigger outburst later on.

HEATING ELEMENT 2: BEING DEFENSIVE

When someone expresses disagreement it is quite hard to address their concerns calmly and objectively in a way that shows an attempt to understand their viewpoint. Instead, people get defensive, which means that they deny any wrongdoing and/or any possibility that they could be contributing to a problem. This creates anger in the other person because they don't feel that they are being listened to.

Cooling element: Counter this by resisting the temptation to get defensive and acknowledging any element of blame, if appropriate.

HEATING ELEMENT 3: MAKING CHARACTER ATTACKS

In a conflict situation it is sensible to restrict your line of argument to what you perceive the other person to have done, rather than attacking their character or personality. Thus, 'When you did this, I felt you were showing me no respect' is more helpful than saying, 'You are so disrespectful.' It is easier to discuss a specific incident without getting angry than when defending oneself against a character assassination.

Cooling element: Avoid making character attacks by sticking to criticism of specific behaviours, not the person's general character.

HEATING ELEMENT 4: OVER-GENERALIZING

Over-generalizing (discussed in chapter 4) can really escalate a conflict and build up the other person's anger. Making sweeping statements can make a small (and perhaps valid) complaint against someone blow up out of all proportion, especially as it is likely to stimulate a defensive reaction in the other person. Using phrases such as 'You always', 'You never' and 'Why do you always have to' lead to sweeping generalizations that fuel the fire of angry conflict.

Cooling element: Avoid over-generalizing by restricting discussion to the issue at hand rather than bringing in old arguments or other simmering resentments.

HEATING ELEMENT 5: NOT LISTENING

As implied earlier, the heat of a conflict can be minimized by really listening to your opponent. This means not interrupting, not rolling your eyes and not being preoccupied by thinking of what you're going to say next. These actions will invariably lead to the other person to feel frustrated and angry that their views are not being taken on board.

Cooling element: Show that you are listening and reflect back to demonstrate genuine understanding.

HEATING ELEMENT 6: BEING RIGHT

In times of conflict, you may well be right and the other person wrong. However, proving that you are right will not necessarily cause the other person to calm down and apologize; on the contrary, as the earlier sections in this chapter have shown, losing face and feeling embarrassed about being wrong can make someone even angrier. It might be better to resist the urge to prove your point in order to win a better outcome.

Cooling element: resist the urge to prove that you are right!

· ·
Quick fix
Winning the argument, being right, or proving your point, won't necessarily be effective in diffusing anger in other people; sometimes there are better longer-term gains to be made by 'giving in' on the need to win.
· ·

HEATING ELEMENT 7: BLAMING

This is similar to trying to prove you are right (above); trying to lay the blame for the disagreement at the feet of the other person might be (in your eyes) correct, but is only going to make that person angrier as they feel wronged and frustrated. Quite often, in conflict situations, both parties can take some blame or accept some responsibility and doing so does not make you appear weak. On the contrary, accepting criticism or blame is the first step to negotiating a peaceful compromise (see below).

Cooling element: Try to counter this by being careful not to blame the other person – try to keep things as neutral as possible.

Heating vs cooling elements

For this exercise you will need to consider a recent conflict situation you have been involved in that escalated into an angry incident. If you can't think of a suitable incident, wait until one arises before completing this exercise.

Consider the incident and identify the elements that might have contributed to the conflict escalating into a full-blown row. As we have seen, heating elements are the things we do that can cause conflict to escalate, while cooling elements are the counter behaviours that can help a conflict cool down somewhat.

Heating element	Example	Cooling element I could have replaced it with
Trying to avoid the conflict		
Being defensive		
Making character attacks		
Over-generalizing		
Not listening		
Being right		
Blaming		

Conflict styles

During the 1970s Kenneth Thomas and Ralph Kilmann researched and identified five main styles of dealing with conflict. These styles vary in their degree of co-operativeness (the extent to which a person wants to satisfy the other person's concerns) and assertiveness (the extent to which a person wants to satisfy their own needs). Thomas and Kilmann argued that people generally adopt a preferred conflict resolution style, even though this might be useful only in some situations and not in others. They developed the Thomas-Kilmann Conflict Mode Instrument (TKI), which many practitioners use to help identify your preferred conflict style.

> **Myth buster**
> It is often assumed that there is one optimal style for dealing with conflict, but the truth is that different styles work well in different situations and at different times.

Thomas and Kilmann's five conflict styles are:

1 Competitive
People who tend towards a competitive style are assertive but uncooperative – they take a firm stand. They usually operate from a position of power by virtue of their rank, expertise or persuasive ability. During a conflict, this person pursues their own concerns without regard for the other person, drawing on their power to help them to win.

This style is good to adopt when there is an emergency and a decision needs to be made fast, or when defending against someone who is trying to exploit a situation for their own ends. However, in other situations it can leave people feeling dissatisfied and resentful.

2 Collaborative

People tending towards a collaborative style try to meet the needs of all people involved and this style is both assertive and co-operative. Collaborative people can be very assertive but, unlike the competitor, they are far better at co-operating and acknowledging that everyone is important; they work to find a solution that meets the needs of all parties, not just their own.

This style is a good one to adopt when you need to bring together a variety of viewpoints to get the best solution, when there are competing demands on few resources, or when the situation is too important for a simple compromise.

3 Compromising

People who prefer a compromising style try to find a solution that will at least partially satisfy everyone. The compromising style is neither very assertive nor very co-operative. Everyone is expected to give up something. Compromising means splitting the difference or accepting the middle ground and can leave no party particularly happy.

Compromise is useful when the cost of conflict is higher than the cost of losing the argument, or when the argument has reached a standstill.

4 Accommodating

This style is about meeting the needs of others rather than their own. There is an element of self-sacrifice and even martyrdom in this conflict style. This person is not assertive but is highly co-operative – the very opposite of competitive. The accommodating person might give in, do what the other person wants and obey orders.

Accommodating is appropriate when the issues matter more to the other party than to you, when you know you are wrong, when you want to create goodwill and build future relationships, or when a peaceful solution is more important than winning the argument.

Sometimes, the accommodating style can be deliberately adopted in order to court favour later on: you give in on this occasion in the hope of winning a different (and more important) battle later. The problem with this strategy, of course, is that the other party may fail to return the favour.

5 Avoiding

Avoiding is unassertive and uncooperative. People tending towards this style try to evade conflict entirely. They don't seek resolution for their own concerns or for those of the other person. Avoiding people might delegate controversial decisions to other people or just sidestep the issue.

This style might work when you know you can't win or when the conflict is really over something not worth bothering about. However, adopting this approach can make you seem weak and ineffectual – and can create resentment and frustration in the other person.

Style	Assertive?	Co-operative?
Competitive	Yes	No
Collaborative	Yes	Yes
Compromising	No	No
Accommodating	No	Yes
Avoiding	No	No

Quick fix
A collaborative style of conflict resolution is the best style to aim for in most situations and allows you to be both assertive and co-operative, which is more likely to diffuse anger.

Once you understand the different styles, you can use them to think about the most appropriate approach (or mixture of approaches) for the conflict situation in which you find yourself. The following exercise should help you learn to do this.

Conflict style diagnostics

Answer the following questions to help you work out whether you are typically using the most appropriate conflict style.

Questions	If you answer yes...
Do you feel that other people rarely listen to your ideas or contributions? Do you feel that others don't respect your views?	You might be using the accommodating style too much in conflict situations.
Do you find it hard to get on with people after conflict situations? Do other people often see you as inflexible or unreasonable? Do you find it hard to admit when you are wrong?	You might not be using the accommodating style enough in conflicts that you have.
Do you find people tending to agree with whatever you say? Do people seem resentful of you?	You might be using the competing style too much.
Do you feel that you have little power during conflict? Do you worry excessively about what other people think of you?	You might be using the competing style too little during conflict resolution situations.
Are you more concerned with keeping people happy than with getting the best outcome? Do you feel that no one is ever happy at the end of any conflict that you are involved in?	You might be using the compromising style too much.

Questions	If you answer yes...
Do you find bargaining or haggling difficult? Do you resent having to give in on a stance you have made?	You may be using the compromising style too infrequently.
Do you prefer to keep the peace at whatever the cost? Do you hate conflict situations and try to avoid them?	You may be over-reliant on avoiding strategies during conflict.
Are you like a dog with a bone – once you have got your teeth into something, you won't let it go? Do you feel it is important to win (or at least defend) every argument, no matter how trivial?	You might not be using avoidance strategies enough – sometimes they are useful.
Do you find that you spend too much time negotiating solutions during conflict? Do you sometimes find that quick outcomes of conflict are just too hard to achieve?	You might be using the collaborating style a little too often.
Is the winning of the argument the most important outcome? Do you like to 'get one over' the other party during conflict situations?	You might not be using the collaborative style enough.

Lloyd's story

Lloyd owns his own removals firm and is aware that he has 'issues' with anger management. The problem for him isn't so much his own anger but how he responds to the anger of other people, both at work and away. He always thinks that if no one got angry with him, he wouldn't get angry back! His problem, he realizes, is that he always goes into competitive or avoidance mode – either determined to win and prove his point, or just walking away.

One day, Lloyd and his colleague move a bulky sofa for a customer, bringing it to the customer's home from a store. But, try as they might, they cannot get the sofa through the doorway of the house. The customer becomes irate and demands that they take the sofa back to the store. The problem is that if Lloyd does this, he won't get paid for the two hours already spent on the job. Lloyd starts getting angry back, blaming the customer for not checking whether it would fit and threatening just to leave it and walk away. The customer starts getting very angry about it being dumped in the hallway and they seem to reach a stalemate.

Lloyd takes a deep breath and decides to adopt a more collaborative approach and stop trying to win the argument. He tells the customer that he will work out a solution and promises not to walk away. The client calms down a bit at this reassurance and Lloyd starts to think more creatively. Eventually, he offers two solutions: one is to take the sofa through the back door, which will involve several steps and extra manpower (and more costs). The other is to remove the door to get the sofa in (and Lloyd will put it back on at no extra charge).

When the client sees that Lloyd is trying hard to come up with a solution, he becomes calmer. He agrees to the door being removed and all goes well – he even gives Lloyd extra money for his efforts even though he hasn't asked for it.

Using communication techniques to reduce conflict

A large part of the conflict style you adopt is tied up with the communication styles and techniques you use. Once you find yourself in a conflict situation with someone, it is important to reduce the emotional charge from the event because it is this emotion that is fuelling the anger within the situation.

A number of communication techniques can be used to prevent anger escalating during a conflict situation. Some of these are outlined below.

AGREEING

The other person might well be angry and armed with a number of arguments accusing you of doing things to cause the problem. When somebody is this angry, they are likely to be beyond reason, so there is little point wasting time and energy in trying to address their arguments. Certainly, when they are so angry, offering a defence is only likely to stoke their anger and make things worse.

To address the other person's anger, then, try to diffuse it by simply agreeing with them. You might be able to do this by finding some truth in their argument (even if you don't agree with everything they say). When you do this, it takes the wind out of their sails and makes it very hard for them to continue to feel and maintain such intense anger.

For example: 'You have no right to expect me to do everything in this house! It's just not on! I am not your slave! I am your daughter! Why should I have to wash up?'

Response: 'You are right. I should not expect you to do everything and I certainly don't think you are my slave.'

Myth buster
Agreeing with or even apologizing to an angry opponent is not about 'giving in'; nor is it a sign of weakness. It is an effective strategy for taking the heat out of an angry situation and should be regarded as a show of strength.

In the example, the responder is agreeing with what they can, while not responding to the parts that they don't feel they can agree with (the issue of the daughter doing the washing up).

If you really don't feel that there is any part of the accusation that you can truthfully agree with, you can at least acknowledge that different people have different ways of seeing things. Agreeing, then, is not about compromising your principles, but about showing that you understand where the other person is coming from. It is aimed at taking the heat out of the flame of their anger.

USING 'I' STATEMENTS

As discussed in chapter 4, using 'I' (e.g. 'I feel') rather than 'you' (e.g. 'You have made me feel...') statements means that you are taking responsibility for yourself and your reactions rather than ascribing blame to the other person for how you feel. This decreases the chance that the other person will become defensive and even angrier. For example, saying 'I feel so upset that I am being accused of such a thing' is less likely to escalate the anger than saying 'You have really upset me.'

STROKING

This is about giving positive strokes, even if the other person is angry and insulting you. By strokes, we mean saying things that are the equivalent to a nice, warm stroke – positive things that make the other person feel good about themselves. For example, 'I am so glad you have raised this with me rather than just letting it fester. I think this shows that you really want to sort this out and move on.'

> **Point to remember**
>
> Trying to find something positive to say about the angry person can really take the wind out of their sails and burst the bubble of anger!

USING THE 'NO-BLAME' APPROACH

The no-blame approach tries to take the sting out of a conflict by removing assignments of blame. Much angry conflict is tied up with the idea that one party has injured the other, so try to steer the attacks away from the personal and avoid discussions about who did what and when.

USING EMPATHY

Putting yourself into the shoes of the other person can help you to choose a communication style that will prevent the anger from escalating. Empathy is an important listening technique – when we are in conflict and dealing with angry people, it is too easy not to listen properly while we consider our own defences or how we are going to respond. Empathy is listening in a way that gives the other person feedback that he or she is being heard and that you understand their position (see the earlier case study about Jenny's experiences).

There are two main forms of empathy:

▶ **Message empathy** is about showing that you understand the point that the other person is making. This can be achieved by reflecting back what they have said; for example, 'I understand that you are really angry because you feel that you have been let down again.'

▶ **Feeling empathy** is about showing that you understand how the other person feels (acknowledging emotion, as referred to earlier). Be careful, however, not to become an amateur psychologist and start ascribing feelings to the other person that you have no evidence they are experiencing. For example, if your friend is angry because you kept them waiting, don't over-analyse by suggesting that 'I understand that you are feeling angry probably because it reminds you of how your dad let you down as a child.' Instead, simply say, 'I understand that being left waiting in a busy pub might make you feel embarrassed and disrespected.'

> ### Point to remember
>
> Showing that you understand what the other person is saying as well as how they feel can help defuse anger effectively.

Using communication techniques

For the following conflicts, decide how you might be able to use each of the above communication techniques to reduce the anger of the other person. Use a table like the first one – which is done for you – for each scenario.

A Your flatmate is furious with you because you finished off the milk again this morning *and* rushed out of the house without washing up your breakfast things. A row starts to escalate, with each of you accusing the other; after all, your flatmate isn't exactly an angel themselves – they rarely do the washing up and leave plates all around the house. How can you defuse the conflict here before it gets out of hand?

Communication technique	How could this be used?
Agreeing	I could agree with them and say 'You are right – I was just wrong on both counts.' This would be better than trying to defend myself (e.g. 'What about the time when you left *me* no milk?', or 'I was in such a rush!').
Using 'I' statements	Instead of accusing my flatmate of being a slob or being too precious over the milk, I can say, e.g. 'I feel frustrated when you leave your plates lying around the house.'
Stroking	I can find positive things to say, e.g. 'You are a great flatmate on the whole' or 'I enjoy sharing a house with you.'
Using the no-blame approach	Instead of perpetuating the cycle of blame (you say I did this, I say you did that, etc.) I will stop accusing and counter-blaming and try to move the discussion forward, e.g. 'OK, maybe we should set up a fine system for anyone leaving the washing up? All money raised going to wine at the end of each week?'
Using empathy	I could show that I understand what they are saying and how my actions make them feel; 'I do hear you and know I left you short of milk and the house a mess. I am sure that left you feeling really angry and frustrated.'

B You bump into someone in the shopping centre and they drop their bags. They start getting angry with you, complaining that you didn't look where you were going because you were too busy texting on your phone.

C You are at a party and someone you know accuses you of talking about them behind their back. They are angry at the rumours that they are accusing you of spreading. The truth is that you do think this person has behaved badly – hence the gossip – but the situation is getting fraught. How can you defuse the anger?

D You are driving along, minding your own business, when someone starts hooting their horn furiously at you. They seem to be accusing you of having cut in front of them, but you don't think you did anything wrong. You don't let it bother you, but when you park at your destination and get out of the car, you notice that your accuser has followed you and is now standing there, angrily berating you. How can you defuse this situation?

MOVING ON

In this chapter you have learned how to recognize and deal with other people when they are angry. You now know how to spot the seven 'heating elements' that can escalate conflict; and you have examined different conflict 'styles' and the range of communication techniques you can use to reduce conflict. The skills discussed here should be enough to take you through most general conflict situations. The next two chapters deal with more specific situations: anger in the workplace and angry children at home.

Key points

1 Before attempting to deal with a conflict situation, try to work out the real reason why the other person is expressing so much anger.

2 Be aware of the 'heating elements' that fuel the fire of anger and try to counter them with techniques that will de-escalate the conflict and cool the other person down.

3 Think about the communication style you use when dealing with conflict and adapt it accordingly.

4 Be aware of the conflict style that you typically adopt and consider whether the accommodating, collaborative, co-operative, avoiding or compromising style is appropriate for the situation.

5 There is a lot to remember when dealing with conflict, so don't expect to get it right first time. The best way forward is to focus on a couple of new techniques at a time rather than trying to make too many changes at once.

8

....

Anger management
in the workplace

How do you feel?
Answer 'true' or 'false' to the following statements.

- *I don't think I should be getting angry at work.*   T/F
- *I don't know why my boss gets angry with me.*   T/F
- *My colleagues seem angry with me.*   T/F
- *I worry about handling customer anger.*   T/F
- *I worry about customers getting aggressive.*   T/F

The more 'true' answers you gave, the more useful this chapter will be
to you.

Unsurprisingly, extremes of emotional display are discouraged in the
workplace, as are negative emotions like fear, disappointment and
anger. However, research suggests that emotions like anger, which
organizations try to suppress, don't simply go away. The ability to
defuse aggression and anger – in ourselves, in the boss, in colleagues
and in customers or clients – is therefore a vital skill to learn if we
want to maintain a pleasant working environment.

What makes us angry at work?

> '...45 per cent of us regularly lose our temper at work, while
> 64 per cent of Britons working in an office have had office rage.'
>
> Sunday Times magazine, 18 July 2006

Work is probably the most prescribed arena in terms of which
emotions we are expected to display and which we are expected to
suppress. At home, with our partners, with our friends, even in the
supermarket, we are much freer to express our feelings, safe in the

knowledge that our loved ones will put up with it or that we need never see strangers at the supermarket again. At work, however, our relationships are not usually so intimate that our colleagues will put up with outbursts – and, of course, we will see our co-workers again and thus have to live with the consequences of any display of emotion. And intense outbursts of anger are rarely tolerated in most workplaces.

Workplaces are traditionally rational places. Emotional reactions, nuances, hunches, and intuition – none of these are considered to have a part to play in the rational enterprise that we call work. Certainly, emotions are well controlled in most work environments by (usually) unwritten organizational rules called **display rules**; these specify which emotions ought to be expressed and which suppressed.

According to a 1999 report by Donald Gibson of Fairfield University and Sigal Barsade of Yale University, one in four employees is substantially angry at work, with half claiming to feel at least 'a little angry' at work. This anger, they suggest, leads to a sapping of energy and job satisfaction at work. My own research suggests that anger is the most commonly *suppressed* negative emotion at work, suppressed in around 10 per cent of all workplace interactions. Some of the more common things that make us angry at work include:

- ▶ others stealing our ideas
- ▶ not being consulted or involved in decisions affecting us
- ▶ practical problems that block our goals, such as parking difficulties or the daily commute
- ▶ colleagues letting us down
- ▶ business contacts not returning our calls
- ▶ technological failures such as computer crashes
- ▶ malicious gossip
- ▶ unfair treatment such as in the type or quantity of work allocated to us
- ▶ a feeling of betrayal by the organization.

We have already discussed our general right to be angry in chapter 4, but we are now looking at specific rights to be angry at work. This is important because many people (especially more passive people) feel that they have to suppress any anger at work – and this suppression can lead to outbursts of displaced anger elsewhere. We are entitled to be angry at work at times and, in fact, it may even be beneficial for us to get angry.

According to a Harvard Medical School study, workers who repress frustration are three times more likely to say they had reached a glass ceiling. The study, which followed 824 people over 44 years, pointed out that while outright fury was destructive, getting angry at work could have its benefits. Lead author Professor George Vaillant said in a BBC report: 'Negative emotions such as fear and anger are inborn and are of tremendous importance' in the workplace because they help people stand their ground and be assertive, which helps them get respect at work.

Adapted from BBC News website, 2 March 2009

Point to remember

Being angry at work can sometimes be beneficial for our career development and in terms of gaining respect from other people; the key is not to show extreme anger reactions and to keep it appropriate.

Knowing when to get angry – and when not to – is the key here. Understanding 'workplace anger rights' is an important first step:

Anger rights that we all have	Examples
The right to feel angry if I have been unfairly treated	• A colleague criticizes you without justification. • The boss gives preferential jobs to others.
The right to feel angry if my needs (which I have expressed assertively) are ignored	• Colleagues are noisy in the office even when you have asked them to be quieter. • You have repeatedly requested information from colleagues that is not forthcoming.

(contd)

Anger rights that we all have	Examples
The right to feel angry if co-workers let me down	• A colleague fails to pass on a phone message. • A colleague does not pull their weight in the team.
The right to feel angry if a customer is rude to me	• A customer hurls personal insults at you. • A customer swears at you or raises their voice.
The right to feel angry if anyone at work is aggressive towards me	• A colleague shouts at you and makes you feel intimidated. • Your boss swears at you or makes you feel threatened.
The right to express my anger assertively at work	• You tell your co-worker when you are angry. • You explain how a customer's actions make you feel.

Quick fix

The key to anger management at work is knowing when you are entitled to get angry and with whom.

Generally, the reasons why other people at work may get angry towards you tend to fit within a finite number of themes, depending upon whether that other person is a customer, a colleague or the boss.

What makes the boss angry?

A good manager or boss should be able to express their anger assertively and appropriately. Of course, that is not always the case and some bosses do scream and shout. Either way, the boss's anger usually reflects some common themes. If your boss is angry with you, or tends to get angry a lot, ask yourself the following questions:

▶ Has your boss been landed with extra work because of something you did/didn't do?

Linked to this theme is the idea that the boss is going to have to do something to make up for your mistakes. As we all know, an unexpected piece of extra work delays us in either getting on with our own projects or even going home or elsewhere. This is likely to make us stressed, but when there is someone to blame for it, we can turn that emotion into anger and have an outlet for it.

▶ Has something you did/didn't do caused your boss to be embarrassed in front of a client?

Imagine the boss delivering a presentation using data that you have prepared, only for the client to point out that the numbers are wrong. Most people would understand the boss being livid with you. Here, the anger stems from the fact that you have made them look stupid.

▶ Could your boss feel that you have let them down?

A manager can feel let down for a whole range of reasons. For example, you haven't done what they asked you to do, you haven't done a piece of work to their required standard, you haven't met a deadline, the work is inaccurate, or the presentation is poor. The anger can arise from the feeling that their wishes are being ignored, that they are not being attended to or listened to properly or from a perception that you are just incompetent (incompetence in others is often a source of anger).

▶ Could your boss feel that you have shown them disrespect?

This source of anger is common with a boss who is a little insecure about his/her own abilities, power and self-efficacy as a manager. They feel that they have to assert themselves as 'the boss' and are sensitive to any apparent attempts to undermine their authority or usurp their power base. Thus, if you do not behave exactly as required, the anger stems not from frustration at having to redo work or disappointment at being let down, but from the fury of what they see as your doubting or weakening their role as manager. In other words, for these threat-sensitive individuals, your inaccurate or late report reflects a lack of respect for them and their authority.

MANAGING THE BOSS'S ANGER

Many of the techniques suggested in chapter 7 can work for the angry boss too. However, in this case there is the issue of power and the power imbalance. While you can always walk away from an abusive customer, or feel reassured that once the encounter is over you need never interact with that person again, the same cannot be said for the angry boss. Here is someone who holds power over you and with whom who you wish to nurture an ongoing relationship. Dealing with their wrath, then, has to be done in such a way as to allow that relationship to continue undamaged.

Adapt the techniques from chapter 7 for handling the angry boss in the following ways:

1 Apologize.
This should not be too difficult to do if you were in the wrong, but it does involve some loss of face. Many workers feel that they have to bluff their way through mistakes for fear that admission of guilt will damage a good impression or reputation. They feel that they must deny the mistake or attempt to shift the blame elsewhere in order to keep in the boss's good books. However, it is more likely that the boss will see through these attempts and be disappointed in you that you are unable to admit your error. Humans make mistakes and managers are often more impressed by a frank and apologetic admission than pathetic attempts to blame-shift.

Myth buster
Apologizing to the boss if you have done something wrong is not a sign of weakness or a sycophantic measure. It can be a reasonable way of clearing up a source of anger between you.

2 Diffuse the anger with agreement.
Nothing disarms the angry person more than complete concurrence. Disagreement fuels anger; when you disagree, the angry person gets more and more frustrated and irritated by their failure to 'get through' to you. By agreeing, the rage dissipates, as they have no one to rant against. This technique is especially effective if the boss is especially furious and beyond reason.

'You are right, I should have been more careful with the figures. I should have double-checked them before I gave them to you. I can't apologize enough.'

3 Offer explanations but not excuses.
This should not be used when the manager's anger is at its peak, but only when s/he is beginning to calm down somewhat. It could

perhaps follow an apology. Explanations are very important and, as humans, we have a need to know why: why something has gone wrong or why something has happened. Offering an explanation is a vital part of the anger diffusion process, but if it sounds as if you are making excuses, this can fuel the rage further. You could say,

'What I did was unforgivable and there is no excuse. However, could I just explain how it happened?'

4 Acknowledge the emotions.

Anger is unlikely to be the only emotion that your boss is experiencing. They may be feeling embarrassed because of the poor impression created to a client by your mistake. Or they could be feeling disappointed or let down, or even stressed at the extra work your mistake has caused. It is important, therefore, to acknowledge how they might be feeling to show that you do understand the consequences of what you have done.

'I must have really embarrassed you by getting those figures wrong – I hope you told them it was me, not you, who messed up?'

5 Reassure the insecure boss.

The boss who feels that your actions reflect a lack of respect for them or their position needs reassuring that this is not the case. This kind of boss may think:

'This person does not listen to me. They don't do as I ask, but they simply ignore my attempts to manage them. Am I such a poor manager?'

These kinds of beliefs can lead to the boss lashing out even more in an attempt to exert authority and control, so it is important to offer the reassurance that is craved:

'It must seem like I'm not listening to you or taking any notice of you. But it's not like that at all.'

6 Suggest ways to repair the damage/make amends.

The final strategy is to offer a solution or some way of making amends. This could involve your redoing the figures or the report, contacting a client to apologize personally, or offering to work weekends.

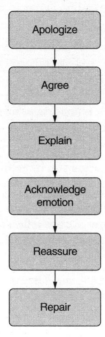

Steps in handling an angry boss

Why do colleagues get angry?

Again, the anger of those you work with is likely to fall within certain themes. Ask yourself the following questions if you find that your colleagues are often angry with you.

▶ Does your colleague feel that you are getting benefits denied to them? These benefits could be anything from extra pay or perks to just being treated with more leniency by the boss. It could be that you are on a higher pay point but that your co-workers do not feel this is justified. Your boss may tolerate late work from you more than from them. Even the perception that the boss likes you more than them can create resentment and anger.

▶ Does your colleague feel that you are not pulling your weight? If co-workers feel that, for whatever reason, you are not co-operating as you should or pulling your weight within the team, this can make them angry. It could be that you have genuine reasons such as absence from work due to ill health and the perception of you may or may not be justified. Even so, the anger stems from the fact that your colleagues will have to work extra hard or extra hours to make up for the loss of your input. There may even be resentment that their extra input will not receive any extra credit, or a feeling that you are 'getting away' with slacking.

▶ Have you made a mistake that has caused your colleague problems?
This could range from failure to deliver an important telephone message to giving inaccurate information in a report. Their anger may stem from a feeling that you have either been too careless, incompetent or perhaps even deliberately attempting to sabotage. These perceptions may be unjustified but remember that, when the heat rises, rationality is reduced.

▶ Have you ignored office etiquette?
The final theme is bound up with office etiquette and can include things such as you 'borrowing' items from your co-workers' desk (staplers, pens, etc.) and not returning them, leaving the photocopier out of paper or failing to report a fault with it, eating noisy or smelly food in a shared office, engaging in loud personal telephone calls or continually trying to chat when they are attempting to work. All these are sources of irritation, but can quickly lead to full-blown anger.

According to a BBC News Online report (14 September 1999), what makes us most angry at work is not the boss or even a heavy workload, but other people gossiping, talking loudly or even making coffee only for themselves. These findings were based on a survey of 1,000 office staff by Office Angels and, of those questioned, 60 per cent said their irritation began with colleagues not bothering to say good morning. Other sources of irritation included colleagues not turning their mobile phones off in meetings, making the office kitchen untidy and leaving a broken photocopier or printer for someone else to fix.

MANAGING YOUR COLLEAGUE'S ANGER

In many cases you may feel that there is no justification for a colleague to be angry with you; however, even in these circumstances, the onus may still be on you to defuse the situation, if only to make a more pleasant working environment. These tips should help:

1 Ask them why they are angry. Too often, we don't really know what is eating our colleagues or are unaware of what we have done to cause offence. Be brave, bite the bullet, and ask.

2 Eliminate or reduce any anger stimulants. Once you have figured out what is making your colleague angry, you will need to eliminate or reduce those sources of anger. This might mean speaking to your boss about altering perceptions of you, it could mean changing your workload or changing the way you behave at work. Of course, this does not mean that you should passively accept any changes demanded of you; any changes you make should be in accordance with your rights, as discussed earlier.

Point to remember

If a colleague appears to be angry with you but you don't know why, try asking them!

Why do customers get angry?

Customers' anger generally falls within the following themes:

▶ Frustration

Customers get angry when they feel that their attempts to get the result they deserve are continually thwarted. Common causes of frustration are automated telephone answer systems (by the time they actually get through to you they may have been hanging on for a long time, been cut off or got lost in the voicemail routing system), being passed from department to department (and often having to explain their situation over and over again) and miscommunication (whereby one person tells them one thing but someone else says something contradictory).

▶ Believing that you don't care or don't care enough

Customers often feel very emotional about trying to achieve what they consider to be a righting of a wrong. That wrong could be anything from receiving damaged or faulty products to poor service, or to more serious concerns such as long hospital waiting lists or a product that has caused some harm or expense (such as the washing machine that damages clothes or a food product that makes someone ill). For you, their problem might be something you have come across dozens of times – just today! It is hard to work up or express the appropriate emotion over and over again, with the consequence that you can come across as bored and uninterested. Nothing is more likely to raise a customer's hackles than the feeling that they are just another complaint to be processed and that nobody cares or even pretends to care.

▶ Believing that you are not doing enough to help

This is similar to the above, but this time the problem is a perceived unwillingness (or lack of ability) to solve the problem. Standard apologies or referring to 'company policy' (e.g. 'It is against company policy to offer reductions to unhappy hotel guests.') are the sorts of processes that make customers feel angry at your apparent refusal to do more to help.

▶ Complicated complaints procedures

Many companies demand that customers write in with complaints, which, in some circumstances, can make customers angry. These include situations when the problem needs solving *now* (a customer who faces missing a flight because check-in has just closed will not be placated by invitations to write in to complain) or when the financial value of the complaint is small (but the principle high). Companies know that most customers are put off by having to write in and this reduces their apparent volume of complaints; however, it can greatly increase anger and frustration among their customer base.

▶ Perception of unjust treatment
The final theme refers to the feeling of being treated unfairly. Customers may feel, rightly or wrongly, that what they are being offered in response to their complaint is unfair. For example, many would get angry at an offer of holiday vouchers as recompense for a ruined holiday, or at an offer of a free film at a photo developing centre in recompense for lost memories. Often the company feels that the customer is being dealt with fairly but the customer does not share that view.

Point to remember

Simply showing that you care and that you understand their problem can often defuse customers' anger. It is indifference that is most likely to inflame rather than defuse a situation.

Why is the customer angry?

Read the following scenarios and note down the reasons why you think each customer is angry.

A Abby's new washing machine has caused her no end of problems. It has never worked properly and repairmen have been sent out three times. Each visit has meant a morning off work for Abby. She has had enough and wants her money back, but she can't seem to get hold of anyone in authority at the customer service number. All anyone can do is keep sending repairmen out. When yet another repairman appears, she starts shouting at him and loses her temper.

B Susie often goes to a particular shopping centre with her toddler because it offers free 'kiddy cars' to borrow. One day she turns up to find that a deposit is now required, despite the fact that she has a special membership card for her son with all her details on it. She doesn't have any spare cash and starts complaining to the customer service person about the new system. The customer service rep scowls and says, 'That's the new rule – if you don't like it, take it up with management, but they won't change it.' Susie feels her hackles rise.

C Pat books into a seaside hotel for the weekend with her family. Unfortunately, the room is very close to the kitchens and the family is kept awake until 2 a.m. by the noise, which starts up again at 6 a.m. She complains the next morning and they are moved to another room, but she is refused a discount for the lost night's sleep they endured – which ruins their day, too, as they are so tired. Apparently, it isn't hotel policy to offer discounts.

MANAGING CUSTOMER ANGER

The customer is possibly the hardest angry person to placate because of the twin demands to both defend your company (or yourself) and obey the adage that 'The customer is king; the customer is always right.' Yet these demands need not be mutually exclusive. An angry customer who is made to feel valued and respected can not only become calm and co-operative but can also become a more loyal customer.

A customer complaint can be seen as an opportunity to deliver outstanding customer service and retain that customer (and their friends/family) for future repeat business. A lot of this is about building on the techniques already presented in this book, but adapting them to the customer's situation. Here's how:

1 Work out which theme the customer's anger fits. Use the section above to identify the source of their anger so that you can deal with it appropriately. Sometimes their irritation might straddle more than one theme. You might need to ask more questions to find out what is really niggling them.
2 Acknowledge that you understand both the problem and the emotion (this is the empathy referred to in chapter 7). This shows that you are listening and understand not only the practicalities of the problem but also how they are feeling about the problem. For example,

> 'So, you've been transferred to voicemail four times, spoken to two other people and you've been cut off once, and this has all taken you two weeks? No wonder you're angry with us!'

3 Very angry people can be beyond rationality, so be wary of asking too many questions at this stage. Making conciliatory or understanding noises is probably the best thing to do: 'I understand,' 'That must have been annoying,' 'That sounds like a real pain,' or 'It sounds like you have been sent on a bit of a wild goose chase there.'

Myth buster
Sometimes, angry customers are beyond rationality so it is not always necessary to offer them explanations. Sometimes just showing sympathy is enough to get them to calm down.

4 Be human. Present a human response. This means expressing sympathy for the caller, rather than just listening like an automated answering service. This might involve a little acting or pretence, but can really help calm the situation.
5 Make out that you care. This can be achieved by giving the customer your name, assuring them that they will not need to do anything else – that you will handle everything from now. This is especially helpful to the customer who has made several attempts to get the problem solved already. Call them by their name. Reassure them that you will get to the bottom of the problem one way or another and make sure you follow this through. Offer to call them back at a later stage to make sure that they are satisfied.
6 Appear to be on their side. A customer is less likely to rant at you if they feel that you are with them. Saying things such as 'We're not normally meant to help in this way, but you've had such a rotten time...', or 'My supervisor asked not to be disturbed but I'll risk it,' can really diffuse their anger with you.
7 Agree with them (if appropriate) and apologize (see chapter 7). It is amazing how hard some people find this. For many angry customers, a genuine apology is all they want. Even better is an assurance that an enquiry into the problem will begin. And even better than all this is an admission, if at all possible, that the customer is right about at least some part of their complaint. 'I can't believe the hassle you have had! You are right to be angry and I am so sorry. I will do whatever I personally can, Mr Smith, to put this right.'

By agreeing with the criticism levelled at you, the customer should be completely thrown. This response is usually the last thing they expect and it can really knock all the fury out of them. It is easy to be angry with someone who disagrees with you but when faced with the 'agreement and apologize' response, the customer is simply disarmed and will usually calm down quickly.

Responding to customer anger

Think back to three instances where a customer has got angry with you – and you don't feel you handled it well. Write down what happened and consider whether you could suggest a better response now.

The incident	A better response?
1	
2	
3	

When customers or clients get aggressive

Angry people do occasionally become aggressive. Managing other people's aggression is rather different from managing anger, simply because of the danger that aggressive people can pose. One of the important aspects of managing a customer's aggression is being aware of when a situation might be getting out of hand. Knowing if and when an angry client is likely to turn aggressive is the key to controlling the situation. Once they have become aggressive, it is harder to manage without resorting to physically restraining techniques (such as calling security to have them ejected from your premises or simply putting the phone down on them).

Spotting the signs of aggression

There are various signs that an angry customer or client might be heading towards aggression.

Carry out this exercise either by thinking back to an aggressive client, or when you are faced with a client who you are worried may become aggressive.

Question	Signs to look for
Has there been any previous aggressive episode?	If you have clients or customers who are known to be aggressive, ensure that you have extra support when faced with such a person.
Can you detect changes in their body language?	Increasing use of fists (e.g. banging on table), pointing or jabbing fingers at you are all signs of increasing aggression.
Is the language being used a warning sign of impending aggression?	Aggressive language that includes threats and insults is an obvious sign of aggression but there are other things to watch out for. Threats and insults are often personal and made against you as an individual, but the aggressor can also show signs of aggression by depersonalizing you and putting you in a group of people against whom s/he has a complaint. Examples might be, 'You lot are all the same...' or 'You lot sit there in your cosy offices and haven't a clue about the real world...'
Does the customer or client appear rational?	When aggression mounts, thought processes become less rational and this produces many signs that the customer or client is 'losing it'. They may repeat things and keep saying the same things over and over again, they may not seem to take in what you are saying or they may talk faster and stumble and stutter over their words more.

Question	Signs to look for
Does the customer or client still have options available to them?	Many people become aggressive when they feel that they have exhausted all other options. Sometimes it is a build-up of sheer frustration that sends them spiralling into aggression but at other times it is a case of them feeling that if they become aggressive they will get the results they demand. It is thus essential never to leave a client with no options open to them (see later).
Do they perceive you as sympathetic?	If the customer or client repeatedly insists that you do not understand their problem, do not understand how they feel, if they maintain that something is simply 'unfair' or continually complain that you are not giving them the information they want, these are all signs that they do not feel that you sympathize with them or appreciate their distress. This can lead them to want to demonstrate to you further just how distressed they are, which usually means some kind of emotional outburst such as tears or rage.

Using language to prevent aggression escalating

Read the following scenario and pick out the language that has caused the customer's anger to escalate.

Jed works in the customer service department of his local post office. One day a very angry man arrives and complains loudly and aggressively about the problems he has had trying to get a parcel delivered. He claims that the postman failed to deliver the parcel twice and pushed a 'You were not home' card through his letterbox – even though he was home on both occasions. The customer claims that the postman didn't even bother ringing the bell to check. He then says that he came to collect the parcel at the post office only to be told he hadn't left the required 24 hours – even though he had. He came back the next day only to be told that his ID wasn't sufficient because the name on the parcel was his wife's. He has now come back a third time, only to be informed by Jed that the parcel has been returned to sender.

Jed can see that the man is getting aggressive and this is how he reacts:

'Look, just calm down, mate, you're not going to get anywhere by shouting the odds like this. Just stop shouting or I will call security and have you removed. Now, with respect, as I keep telling you, we are only following standard procedure so it's really not our fault. It is against company policy to allow people to collect mail without proper ID – as I have been telling you for about ten minutes now, if you would just stop shouting and listen! Now, there is really nothing else you can do – the parcel has gone back to the sender so you will just have to take it up with them.'

Did you spot the common errors that Jed made? See below for the answers.

It is extremely easy to 'wind up' an angry person further by the words and phrases that you use. When that angry person is also aggressive, it is vital not to do this. Using key words and phrases could make your client/customer/patient more aggressive when your goal is to get them to become less aggressive. Here are some of the key things that Jed should have avoided:

'Look, just calm down (1), mate, you're not going to get anywhere by shouting (2) the odds like this. Just stop shouting or I will call security and have you removed. Now, with respect (3), as I keep telling you (4), we are only following standard procedure so it's really not our fault. It is against company policy to allow people to collect mail without proper ID – as I have been telling you for about ten minutes now, if you would just stop shouting and listen! Now, there is really nothing else you can do (5) – the parcel has gone back to the sender so you will just have to take it up with them.'

1 **Never tell them to calm down.** Of course this is exactly what you want them to do, but saying this is almost guaranteed to fuel their fury. There are a number of reasons for this. First of all, if they are not calm, that means that they have probably lost reason and rationality so are likely to deny that they need to calm down ('I am perfectly calm!' they may shout.) Secondly, to them you are avoiding the issue that is making them angry in the first place ('Don't tell me to calm down, just do what I want!'). Instead of asking them to calm down, then, use more precise language; for example, 'Please talk in a softer voice.'

2 **Avoid saying things like 'You're not going to get anywhere by shouting.'** People often become aggressive when they feel that all their options are exhausted, so saying this to them will further frustrate them and make them even more prone to aggression.

3 **Avoid patronizing language.** Phrases such as 'With respect...' can be seen as patronizing but there are other ways to be patronizing; many people when faced with angry customers tend to repeat the same thing over and over again as if they cannot get their message through (for example, repeating the mantra 'That is against company policy' every time the person requests something); another patronizing technique is to say things very slowly as if dealing with a child. All these things can cause aggression to escalate.

4 **Avoid repeating yourself too much.** One assertive language technique is the 'broken record', which involves simply restating the facts or repeating the message over and over. However, be wary of this when faced with someone who is aggressive. Use of this technique here can cause aggression to escalate as it just increases their frustration.

5 **Avoid dead-end statements.** These serve to signify to the customer that either there is nothing more they can do or that you are not prepared to help them any more. You might want to do this to get rid of them and end the conversation, but the customer is then left with no options and this can breed aggressive reactions. Common dead-end statements include:
   ▷ 'There's nothing more I can do.'
   ▷ 'You can't speak to my manager and, anyway, he would say the same.'
   ▷ 'There's no one else you can speak to.'
   ▷ 'It's against company policy.'
   ▷ 'You can write to Head Office but they will say the same.'

Techniques to defuse aggression

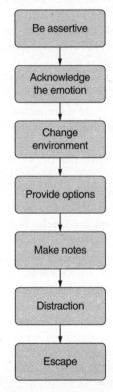

Defusing aggression step by step

1 Be assertive (see chapter 4).

This means telling the aggressor that their actions are not acceptable – and, if appropriate, why not – and giving them an alternative way of behaving. For example, 'Shouting is not acceptable. You are disturbing other people and making me feel uncomfortable. Please speak more quietly.' If you were just to ask them to stop shouting without providing an alternative, they would probably immediately shout back 'I'm not shouting!' Don't say 'please' too much, though, as this can make you appear more passive than assertive.

2 Acknowledge the emotion (see chapter 7).

Aggression often escalates when people feel they are not being understood, at least in the terms of the way they feel. It is thus important to show that you understand or accept their feelings. Examples might be, 'I understand that you are really upset at having missed your flight,' or 'I can see that you are very angry.' Although such statements are likely to see an initial flurry of further rage ('Of course I'm angry – what are you going to do about it?'), continued efforts to demonstrate your understanding should pay off because it can send the message that their anger (but not their aggression) is understandable and even acceptable.

3 Change the environment (see chapter 7).

If possible, try to get the aggressor to a new environment. This is especially important if the person is being aggressive in front of others before whom they would lose face by calming down. Also, changing the environment can be a distraction and give time and space for the aggressor to calm down. Of course, you should not place yourself at risk or use physical contact.

The way you request the move (to another office perhaps) has to be handled with care. The aggressor might think you just want to avoid a 'scene' (which they might be keen on making). Suggesting that the complaint is serious enough to warrant special attention is the best way to deal with this. For example, 'I can see how angry you are and I want to help you. Let's go into my office where I will be able to get access to the extra information I need.'

4 Give them options.

As mentioned before, people are more likely to get aggressive when they feel that they have reached the end of the road and there are no alternatives left. Meeting a brick wall of resistance is frustrating for anyone, and even more so for those who have difficulty controlling their anger. Instead of using dead-end statements (see above) with aggressive people, do all you can to assure them that they have not reached the end of the road (even if they have).

Take care here: someone who has been given a dead-end statement who then turns aggressive should not be suddenly told that there is now something that can be done for them after all. It is obviously not a good idea to backtrack and appear to reward the aggression (especially in view of other customers). Instead, it might simply be a case of giving them the options available, even if they are not desirable ones. For example, you could give them the name and address of the customer service manager at Head Office or a complaints form (always better than just vaguely telling them to write to Head Office), you could offer to go and 'check' with your superiors, or you could repeat any earlier offers to solve the problem.

5 Make notes.
It is amazing how powerful the simple act of scribbling furiously in a notebook can be. It is an act that sends the message that you take the person seriously, they are being listened to and that their comments and complaints will be passed on. It is also a useful way of telling an aggressor that any abuse will be recorded. (Do be careful that they do not think that the notes are only for recording abuse, as this can increase anger, not decrease it.)

6 Use distraction techniques.
It might sometimes be possible to draw the aggressor into a conversation about something else related to the problem but less confrontational (see the following case study for an example).

7 Leave the situation.
This could mean bringing the conversation to a temporary or permanent close. You can tell aggressive callers on the phone that you are going to check something out and will 'get back to them'. Whether you do or not depends on just how aggressive or abusive they have been. You can end face-to-face contacts by making excuses such as, 'I will just go and get my notebook/laptop.' A temporary break in the conversation can give the client time to reflect on their position and calm down on their own. It can also give you time to take stock and decide what to do next.

166

Susie's story

Susie is a hospital receptionist in Accident and Emergency. A patient, furious to be kept waiting, approaches her and aggressively demands to know when a doctor will see him. Susie asks him if he has ever been to this A&E department before and, somewhat taken aback by the direction of her conversation, he says that he hasn't but that he has been to another department. 'What was the wait like there?' she asks. 'Just as bad,' he replies angrily, 'I had to wait two hours to have my chest seen to.' He then goes on to tell her that his grandson accompanied him that time – a piece of information that gives Susie the chance to lead him on to less confrontational topics. She asks after his grandson – 'Is he at work now?' – and lets him talk about the boy for a while. This calms the patient down and distracts him from his complaint enough to listen to Susie's explanation of why he has been waiting so long.

Dealing with the aftermath of aggression

An aggressive episode at work can have a significant psychological impact on you by leaving you feeling stressed and/or angry. Use the following checklist after an aggressive episode to help you understand your reactions.

Aggression aftermath checklist

Do you feel:	Y/N

- anger towards the perpetrator about the abuse you have experienced?
- resentment towards your organization, which has put you in this position and which you may feel has not given you adequate protection?

(contd)

- resentment towards colleagues or managers who were not there when needed?
- regret that you did not handle things differently?
- fear about the way things may have turned out?
- the need repeatedly to go over the episode in your mind, reliving what happened and what might have happened?
- an increased vulnerability not just in your place of work but in other situations too?
- a heightened sense of awareness about the perceived risk of situations?

All these are normal reactions in the immediate aftermath of an aggressive episode and can last days or weeks, depending on the severity of the episode (and on the makeup of the 'victim'). The psychological impact can be managed by taking the following steps:

▶ Accept that you might well experience the emotions outlined above. Acknowledge that these are normal reactions and that they will dissipate with time.
▶ Have some sort of outlet for your feelings. This could be writing down what happened and how you felt, or talking to colleagues or friends. This is healthier than bottling it up.
▶ Your organization should have some sort of incident procedure for reporting and dealing with incidents like this. Good procedures include debriefing (perhaps by counsellors) as well as measures to consider the antecedents, behaviour and consequences of the event in order to reduce the risk of it either happening again or having the same impact. If your organization does not have such procedures (perhaps because the incident was so unexpected), you perhaps you could use your experiences to do something positive by helping develop better procedures (including risk assessment).

MOVING ON

Workplace anger is an issue that affects most of us at some point in our working lives and this chapter has outlined the various methods of anger management to use with colleagues, the boss and with customers and clients.

Key points

1 It is not only OK, but sometimes advisable, to get angry in the workplace; the key is to know when it is appropriate to do so.

2 If the boss is angry with us, finding out why and what we can do about it is the key towards managing it; never just ignore it and hope it blows over.

3 Colleagues get angry with us for a range of reasons, some of which may seem trivial, but understanding and addressing their concerns will make for much better relationships at work.

4 Customer anger is hard to deal with because of the power imbalance arising from the idea that 'The customer is king'. However, careful consideration of the reasons for a client's anger can lead to its successful management.

5 Customers rarely get aggressive suddenly; there are usually signs that someone is about to become aggressive. Looking out for these signs can help minimize the chances of a client's anger exploding into something more threatening.

9

When our children are angry

How do you feel?
Answer 'true' or 'false' to the following statements.

- *I am afraid of my child getting angry.* T/F
- *I tend to do things to avoid making my child angry.* T/F
- *I get upset when my child gets angry.* T/F
- *I get angry when my child gets angry.* T/F
- *I feel that my child's tantrums are a reflection of my parenting ability.* T/F

The more 'true' answers you gave, the more likely it is that your reactions to your child's or children's anger is actually fuelling the problem and making things worse. This chapter aims to help you get your children to manage their own anger and to help you manage your own anger when interacting with your children.

Why do children get so angry?

'Temper tantrums are both prevalent and frequent in young children and they often present a serious management problem for their parents.'

J.A. Green and P.G. Whitney, 2011

We all love our children, but they seem designed to make us angry at times! Not only that, but they have limited ability to control their own anger, which means that they seem to get angry all the time – which makes us even angrier. What can be done to break this vicious cycle?

Children get angry for all sorts of reasons, some of which are the same as for adults and some of which are very different. In general, they tend to get angry when:

- ▶ they feel misunderstood
- ▶ they feel that they are the victim of injustice
- ▶ they feel unfairly treated
- ▶ their goal is thwarted (i.e. they don't get want they want).

Carol Tavis, in her book *Anger: The Misunderstood Emotion* (1989), sees children's tantrums as following a circular pattern, as follows:

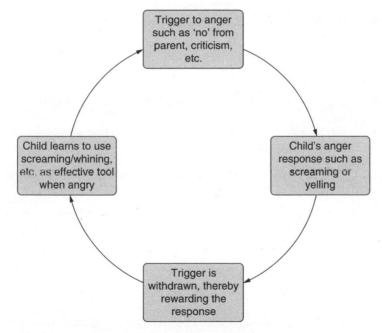

The cycle of anger in children

Breaking this cycle is the key to the effective management of your child's anger outbursts. Obviously, toddlers get angry for different reasons than older children and teenagers and need handling differently. This section will examine the best ways to deal with anger for three age groups:

▶ toddlers and young children (aged 2–4)
▶ older children (aged 5–12)
▶ teenagers.

Dealing with toddler anger

Toddlers are emerging out of babyhood and are trying desperately to assert their independence as they learn new skills. The most common reasons for their anger are likely to be:

▶ frustration: they can't do something either because they are not capable or because an adult is preventing them
▶ delayed gratification: they want something and they want it now!
▶ testing your boundaries: how far can they push you?
▶ tiredness, hunger or thirst: they don't know how to convey this appropriately
▶ too much stimulation: they are overwhelmed by too much going on
▶ manipulation: they are trying to influence you into giving them what they want.

Point to remember

Toddler anger can be a very effective means of manipulating you – if you let it!

Keep a diary of your toddler's tantrums

By keeping a diary of your toddler's tantrums over the course of a week, you will get a better picture of the main issues that lead to angry episodes: the background (e.g. whether they are tired or hungry), how you respond (e.g. whether you shout or give in) and the outcome (how the episode ends or resolves). Fill it in under the headings shown in the following example.

Background	Reason for tantrum	Your response	Outcome
On day trip with whole family including my parents.	Josie wanted an ice cream but I said no because she had already had one that day.	I felt embarrassed and frustrated that my parents would think I wasn't a good mum. I stayed firm but Josie just screamed and yelled.	My dad actually took her and bought her the ice cream!!

Pre-empt tantrums where possible, by making sure the child is not over-tired or overwhelmed and is fed and watered. When toddlers get angry, everyone around them knows it. They express their anger in a totally physical way and almost every part of their body is involved. They might:

- ▶ cry
- ▶ scream
- ▶ stamp their feet
- ▶ lie on the floor
- ▶ kick
- ▶ grimace.

A landmark diary study of children's tantrums (Goodenough, 1931) showed that physical reactions – such as kicking, stamping, jumping up and down, hitting and throwing themselves on the floor – occurred in up to a quarter of tantrums, which might offer some reassurance! Vocal behaviours are more common, with crying, screaming or whining occurring in up to 85 per cent of tantrums. These findings have been replicated more recently (Potegal and Davidson, 2003) in a study of toddlers up to five years old, which found that crying was the most common feature of a tantrum (occurring in 86 per cent of tantrums), followed by screaming and shouting (40 per cent) and finally by whining (13 per cent).

HOW DO YOU FEEL?

When your toddler gets angry, you may feel one or more of the following emotions:

- ▶ embarrassed – what will other people think of my parenting skills?

- angry right back – how dare they do this to me?
- frustrated – everything is such a battle
- depressed – I am such a bad parent
- disappointed – I wanted this day to be so nice
- tired – it's exhausting dealing with tantrums all the time
- afraid – I worry that I won't be able to control my own anger.

So, how to deal, then, with your angry toddler? Your toddler can't help but express their powerful emotions in a physical way as their language skills in general are just not up to it (and nor is their self-control), but it is for the parent to teach them how to manage their emotions more effectively. This requires a calm and supportive approach rather than you shouting or screaming back. You need to offer love, acceptance and reassurance at this stage. After all, your toddler is the one out of control, and needing you to be in control in order to help manage the situation.

> **Quick fix**
> It is essential not to fight anger with anger when dealing with your raging toddler. Instead, fight anger with calm reassurance and love.

TOP TIPS FOR DEALING WITH TODDLER TANTRUMS

1 **Pick your battles.** Toddlers are constantly trying to assert their independence and some battles of wills may just not be worth fighting over. Look through your anger diary and if the reasons for anger tend to be things like your child wanting to wear sandals on a rainy day or go out wearing fairy wings, consider whether these are battles worth fighting.

2 **Don't back them into a corner.** Just like adults, toddlers need an escape route so that they have a dignified way out. For example, 'No, you are wearing the red jumper', leaves nowhere for them to go, but 'You have to wear the red jumper but you can pick which trousers to wear/wear the blue jumper tomorrow', do allow some face to be saved.

3 **Avoid getting into an argument.** Toddlers in a rage are well beyond reason so there is no point in even trying to reason with them.

4 **Don't give as good as you get.** This means not shouting back or losing your own temper. That won't get you anywhere.

5 **Offer unconditional love.** Your toddler needs to feel safe and secure; holding them close and letting them cry can be an effective way to achieve this.

6 **Don't punish them.** They can't help having a tantrum; they really are out of control so it seems unfair to punish them for something they can't help.

7 **Don't give in to their demands.** If you give in you are in effect rewarding them for the tantrum; they will then learn that losing their temper brings results.

8 **Don't be afraid of the tantrum.** Some parents are so afraid of their child's tantrums that they are afraid to say no, but there is no point in walking on eggshells in an attempt to avoid them.

9 **Try ignoring the tantrum.** By praising good behaviour and ignoring the poor behaviour, you don't reward the child for screaming and shouting but for calming themselves down and controlling their emotions; this helps them learn the all-important benefits of self-control.

10 **Find ways to distract them.** Distraction can work very well with this age group; when your toddler is in full flow, try to distract them by either doing something unusual (a dance?) or by offering something different (but not a reward), such as a drink.

11 **Offer a 'time out'.** While the 'naughty step' seems inappropriate for a small child who cannot help their loss of emotional control, quiet time out (away from an audience) can be beneficial. You might have to move them physically to somewhere safe, so do this lovingly, making it clear that it is not a punishment but just a way of allowing them time to calm down on their own (after which they can rejoin you).

Parents often say, 'I feel he's deliberately winding me up' or, 'She knows exactly how to press my buttons.' However, the belief that your toddler is hell-bent on driving you mad for the sake of it is unrealistic because this kind of sophisticated manipulation is developmentally impossible. It requires the child to be able to understand that other people have beliefs and intentions that differ markedly from those of their own. This 'theory of mind' doesn't start to develop until the end of the toddler years, so letting go of this idea that they are 'out to get you' can help you cope with their behaviour better.

Three-year-old Harry is, according to his mother Julie, 'an angry child'. Julie has kept a diary of his tantrums for a week and discovered that he averages 15 a day. One memorable day he notched up 32 separate tantrums. When she looks back at her diary to see why he got angry each time and what her response was, she finds a pattern emerging.

She finds that Harry tended to get angry when he didn't get what he wanted. On Monday he went into meltdown because he wanted to have breakfast before getting dressed, then again because he didn't want to brush his teeth, then again when he wanted to wear a different top (that was in the wash), then again when he wanted sugary 'weekend' cereal for breakfast instead of the healthier weekday kind, and so on.

Julie notices that her responses to Harry's tantrums tended to vary as the day wore on. She started off full of resolve not to give in to him (she has read parenting books!), but by the time he had had his sixth tantrum before 9 a.m., she was exhausted from it all. She feels that he wore her down and, with two other children to cope with, it was easier to give him what he wanted in order to have a bit of peace. She knows she shouldn't have given in but she was just too tired of it all to argue any more.

Julie realizes that her behaviour wasn't consistent and also that she was rewarding Harry for his tantrums. She decides to turn the whole thing on its head and start rewarding him for not having tantrums. She buys a reward chart and explains that every time she tells him 'no' and he reacts without crying and screaming, he will get a star. When he has ten stars he will get a small present. She also starts giving him limited choice for every option, where possible: for example, allowing him to choose whether to brush his teeth before or after getting dressed, or whether to have a banana or an apple as a snack. In addition, she resolves never to give in to a tantrum.

These strategies are successful and Harry's tantrums grow less frequent and less prolonged. He begins to learn self-control, something that he hasn't needed to bother with before. Now he has an incentive for doing so.

Here are two sample star charts you can use to encourage tantrum control in your toddler.

Option 1: a star is earned for every tantrum-free session

	Morning	Afternoon	Evening
Monday			
Tuesday			
Wednesday			
Thursday			
Friday			

Option 2: a star is earned every time the child does not get angry at 'trigger point'

Trigger point	Star?
E.g., being told 'no'	

Quick fix
When dealing with your toddler's anger, be consistent and reward when the anger is being controlled, not when it isn't.

Dealing with older children's anger

As children move out of toddlerhood, they learn to control their anger a little more, but until they are about ten they are still incompetent emotion managers. This means that they are still likely to find it difficult to control and express their anger appropriately. The triggers that make them angry now are fairly similar to those that triggered their anger when they were younger, but their reasoning is a little more sophisticated.

The most common reasons for their anger are likely to be:

▶ perceived injustice: 'It's not fair!'
▶ frustration: being prevented from doing something they feel qualified to do but that the parent feels they are too young for
▶ being told no: while older children can cope better than toddlers with delayed gratification, being told they can't have something still doesn't go down well
▶ being 'made' to do something they don't want to do
▶ boundary testing: this doesn't stop when toddlerhood ends
▶ tiredness: this is still a big factor for older children
▶ manipulation: attempts at manipulation become more sophisticated and can depend on how successful these attempts were when they were younger.

Keep a diary of your child's tantrums

While toddlers can have several tantrums a day (or even an hour), older children tend to have significantly fewer tantrums, though they may last longer. Keeping a diary using a table like the one below can help identify patterns of their anger triggers, which can be a first step to helping you manage their outbursts.

Background	Reason for tantrum	Your response	Outcome

Older children often still lack the ability and self-control to express their anger in appropriate ways. They tend to use the following techniques to demonstrate their injured feelings.

- Sulking
- Screaming
- Shouting
- Crying
- Stamping feet
- Slamming doors
- Hiding in their room
- Refusing to co-operate
- Running away
- Hitting people (especially siblings)
- Throwing things or wrecking their toys

All this is normal, but the trick to managing your child's anger is to start to teach them more effective ways of expressing their emotions and of communicating their distress.

TOP TIPS FOR DEALING WITH YOUR ANGRY CHILD

Examples of creative techniques you can develop with them include the following.

1 Draw or paint
Encourage them to draw or paint a picture to express how they feel – or of what is making them angry. This could be furious black scribbles across the page or a picture of themselves or someone else. Allow them to use as many pages as they wish and to work in privacy if they wish. They may want to tear the page up when they have finished or they may be willing to talk through with you what they have drawn.

2 Use a star chart
Use an anger control star chart (as for a toddler; see above) to reward every half-day that they manage to avoid an angry outburst; this encourages them to develop self-control because they can see an immediate benefit to doing so.

3 Use distraction
Suggest that your child counts to ten (or backwards from ten to one), walks away or uses some other distraction technique when they start smouldering.

4 Spot the warning signs
Help them identify their own early warning signs that their anger is starting to rise and encourage them to nip the anger in the bud before it becomes a fully fledged monster that gets out of control. Early

warning signs include faster breathing, tense muscles and a feeling of distress (but they can vary from child to child).

5 Show affection
Show them that you love them even when they are in the middle of a temper tantrum and telling you that they hate you! Reward your child with your loving attention once they control their anger.

6 Find a physical outlet
Encourage them to do something energetic when they are angry. Take them for some time out while also giving them an outlet for their excess energy by taking them for a walk, a bike ride or a swim. If this is not possible and you are stuck indoors, you could buy them a stress ball to allow some physical outlet for their anger, or even encourage them to run up and down the stairs.

7 Breathe
Teach your child to breathe their anger out. Encourage them to slow their breathing down, take deep breaths, and every time they breathe out they should imagine a little more of their anger leaving their body.

8 Write it down or act it out
Encourage them to write down their feelings either with a diary or just in their own words. Use the template below (you may have to help younger children to write).

Some children can benefit from acting out stories with their toys about what has happened to make them angry; you could even have some special dolls set aside to play with in this way when they get angry.

9 Let rip
Give them a magazine to tear to shreds – that can be a very satisfying way to let rip the anger!

10 Ask questions
Help them work through their feelings by asking them insightful questions about what they are thinking (such as, 'What is it about what happened that is making you so upset? Do you feel that no one is listening to you? Do you feel that we don't care?').

11 Acknowledge the feelings
Accept and acknowledge their feelings rather than trying to dismiss them. 'I don't know why you're so upset, it's only a toy,' is not helpful

and only teaches them that their feelings are inappropriate. Teach them instead that it is OK and normal to feel angry sometimes.

12 Don't belittle
Avoid sarcasm ('Great, you've made a mess yet again!'), threats ('If you don't hurry up, I'll go without you.'), labelling ('You're so slow.') or criticism ('You're taking for ever – what are you, a baby?') when speaking to your child. In the short term these kinds of comments will just provoke your child more and in the long term they may adversely affect their self-esteem.

13 Remind your child that we all get angry
Finally, tell your child that everyone (even you) gets angry. Part of being a good role model is letting your children know that you are susceptible to anger too. Let your child know about a time when you were angry and anger management helped you successfully resolve the problem in a positive way.

Anger template

What happened?	What do you feel?	How angry on a scale of 0–100 do you feel?

Children of this age can benefit from anger management techniques that can be developed when they are not angry. You don't have to wait for them to have a tantrum before working with them on their anger management skills! In fact, it can be much more effective to help them develop self-control, emotional awareness and emotional literacy when they are calm and relaxed, so as to 'inoculate' them against the most severe effects of their feelings during the times when they really feel angry.

Quick fix
Manage your child's anger by spending time helping them develop tools of effective anger management before they actually need them.

Develop your child's' emotional awareness and emotional literacy through the following exercises.

Exercise 1

Encourage your child to comment on other people's emotions as well as their own. This helps your child learn to identify their own feelings and those of other people; to be able to express their emotions effectively, they must first be able to identify them. The more you can encourage your child to express their feelings, the less emotions will build up and overflow into angry explosions. Whenever possible, refer to your own and other people's feelings and guess at, reflect back and question their emotions as well as those of your child.

For example:

'That man in the café seems angry. I wonder what is making him so annoyed?'

'Gosh, did you see how that lady pushed in front of the queue in the supermarket just then? How do you think that made the shoppers in the queue feel?'

'Did you kick your brother because you felt angry that he was trying to get my attention when we were talking?'

Exercise 2

Use role-play to try out various solutions to anger-triggering incidents that might happen to your child. This helps them practise responses to anger-eliciting events, such as 'What would you do if a friend snatched a toy from you?' Suggest suitable responses to replace aggressive or angry ones.

Dealing with anger in teenagers

Many researchers and commentators have tried to look for reasons to explain the British riots in the summer of 2011, but one source believes that at least part of the cause was that young people were 'angry'. The report in *The Guardian* (5 September 2011) suggested that there had been 'simmering anger' for some time before the riots.

The article quoted Dave, 17, who said, 'I'm not saying I know why people kicked off, but I do think most people … and kids are angry, angry about jobs, no housing, no training … just that there's no help, no way to do better.' Dave, claims *The Guardian* piece, knows that 'kids are angry', and that background of anger seems a significant factor when examining the causes of the UK riots.

Another teenager interviewed, 17-year-old Sylvia, pointed out: 'People are angry, some people wanted to get the government to listen, some are angry but don't know why yet … the younger ones, anyway, they've got the same shit to come as us, nowhere to go and it will be worse by the time they're 17 and 18.'

Teen hormones, teen mood swings and teen problems – they are enough to make anyone angry. Angry teens should be considered a normal, if rather unpleasant, part of family life. The problem is that teenagers often no longer look like children, and adults frequently expect a lot from them in terms of their self-control and emotional expression. But anger management is hard enough for many adults, so it is probably unreasonable to expect teenagers to know what to do with their angst and how to express it appropriately.

WHAT DO TEENAGERS GET ANGRY ABOUT?

Teenagers can get angry about anything and everything, including school, teachers, their friends, their siblings and, quite often, their parents. Teenagers are trying to find their place in the world while dealing with issues such as identity, detachment (from parents), the meaning of life, peer pressure and their first romantic relationships – all of which are a lot for anyone to deal with.

Their anger often fits within the themes of perceived injustice and unfairness: for example, teachers who 'pick' on them unfairly, parents who make them wash the dishes when they have better things to do, tests that they performed poorly at because they included 'unfair' questions and so on. Teens may also rally against the unfairness of life as they begin to realize (but not quite accept) that life is unfair. Their lack of height or perceived beauty angers them, as does the lack of money or designer clothes that they feel they are suffering from.

> ## Point to remember
>
> Teenagers are going through a time of major transition and have to cope with a lot of new things at once, such as their changing body, their developing sense of self and their growing independence. Learning to manage and control their emotions is just one more difficult challenge for them.

Other triggers for teen anger include:

- ▶ **habit:** when the young person gets used to a typical pattern of responding
- ▶ **attention seeking:** when the young person uses their anger to get a response
- ▶ **low self-esteem:** when the young person uses anger as a defence mechanism against something that might damage their self-esteem (for example, if they find homework too hard, they might get angry in order to avoid admitting that they can't do it)
- ▶ **criticism:** when the young person's fragile and poorly developed self-esteem means they are very sensitive to criticism.

All this anger can lead young people to feel sad and depressed, especially if they do not express their anger but bottle it up inside. Alternatively, if it isn't bottled up but expressed inappropriately (in temper tantrums or aggressive behaviour), the young person

can be left feeling guilty or embarrassed, which can lead to loss
of confidence and self-worth. This lack of self-esteem can even
lead to addictions – to alcohol, tobacco or illegal drugs. It can
certainly make teenagers intolerant of others (especially their family,
who seem to bear the brunt of much of their anger) and damage
their relationships with parents and others. Excessive anger can
sometimes lead to violent behaviour, either aimed at others (for
instance bullying), or directed against themselves, in the form of
self-harming.

Myth buster
Aggression or self-harm in teens is not a normal part of anger
expression that they will 'grow out of' (though they might), and
indicates a need for expert or professional input.

Angry teenagers 'risking health'

Angry teenagers could be storing up health problems for the future,
according to scientists. A study in the US has found that teenagers
who have problems controlling anger or who suppress angry
feelings are more likely to gain weight. It is thought that overeating
is used by teenagers to anaesthetize their feelings and help suppress
their anger.

Abridged from a BBC news report, 6 March 2004

Your teenager may need expert help with their anger if they get into
fights, get into trouble at school or hurt themselves or other people.
Otherwise, their anger should be considered normal (remember
that feeling angry is not bad – it is what they do with this anger that
is the issue) and you can suggest the following exercises that they
might try.

Anger management for teenagers

If your teen is amenable, you could work through this exercise with
them; if not, encourage them to do it on their own. This exercise
should be carried out while they are calm rather than in the throes
of an angry meltdown.

1 Tune in to your feelings. Note what makes you angry and why. Note that 'It's not fair' is not really an adequate explanation: ask yourself why you feel it's not fair and what, if anything, could reasonably be done to make it fair. Use the following template.

What makes me angry?	Why does it make me angry?	What can I do about this?

2 Recognize and acknowledge your right to be angry – and when you don't have the right to be angry. Add your ideas to the following template.

I have the right to be angry when...	I don't have the right to be angry...
• someone treats me badly	• when I don't get what I want
• I am taken for granted	• when others don't do as I want
• I am treated unfairly	• over every little thing
• I am criticized unfairly	• because the world 'owes me'
• someone is abusive or aggressive towards me	• to get attention
	• to look tough
	• to intimidate someone else

3 Build your self-esteem and self-worth so that you do not feel so sensitive to criticism or injustice. Use the following template to help you.

What things do you do well?
1
2
3
4
5

What achievements have you had?	1
	2
	3
	4
	5
What have you done that was hard to do?	1
	2
	3
	4
	5
What things can you do easily?	1
	2
	3
	4
	5
What evidence is there that people like you?	1
	2
	3
	4
	5
What compliments have you been given?	1
	2
	3
	4
	5
What good things have happened to you?	1
	2
	3
	4
	5

....

4 Finally, think back to an episode that made you really angry and ask yourself the following probing questions to challenge your angry feelings.

Questions	Explanations
Were my thoughts tending to start with words such as 'must', 'should', 'never'?	'He should have done this', 'They never do that'; such absolutes are not helpful and tend to escalate the feeling of anger as they make you feel even more furious at all the wrongs that have been done to you in the past. Better just to concentrate on what happened, not what should have happened or has happened before.
Were my expectations in this episode unreasonable?	This is the million-dollar question – how do you know if they were reasonable or not? Your friends will support you and say they were, but try to take an objective and more distant look at what happened and play 'devil's advocate' by imagining things from other viewpoints.
Was I reacting to hurt, loss or fear?	What, actually, was the reason for your anger? Fear is very common, as is hurt/humiliation. Figure out the real reason behind your outburst.
How did I express my anger?	Was it appropriate? Could there have been another way?
To whom or what was my anger directed?	Was it aimed at the right target? Or could you perhaps have been taking it out on someone or something else?
Did I focus on what had been done to me rather than what I could do to resolve the problem?	It is normal to feel so indignant about what has happened that we fail to concentrate enough on how to solve the problem or resolve the conflict.

How to cope when your children get angry

So far we have looked at how you can help your children manage their own anger, but sometimes it is the parent who needs help in coping when their children get angry. This is often the biggest issue with our children's anger: it is not about helping them to manage their anger, but about helping you as their parent to cope with their anger, especially when it is directed at you.

When children get angry, it is natural for parents to react. If we don't express our anger and we suppress it, it can lead to frustration, resentment, bitterness, a sense of hopelessness and depression, none of which are good things for us or for our children in the long term.

What happened during your childhood?

Think back to your own childhood and consider these questions.

- Did you often get angry as a child?
- Did you have many tantrums or often lose your temper?
- How did those around you react?
- Were you taught to express your anger appropriately?
- Were you taught that it was OK to get angry?
- Did you learn to suppress your anger?
- How did other people, like your parents, express their anger?
- Were you restrained when you got angry?
- Were you punished, distracted or ignored?

The answers to these questions will help you consider your response to your own children's anger.

Maria's story

Maria finds it extremely difficult to cope with her children's tantrums. She has four children, aged from 4 to 14, so she gets both toddler and teen anger. She finds her teenager's anger especially upsetting, as it seems so personal and hurtful. She feels like a terrible mother to induce such rage in her teenaged daughter. Her toddler's tantrums also make her feel bad because they invariably happen in public and she feels sure that everyone is judging her and finding her parenting skills wanting. She doesn't know how to handle the tantrums: she thinks that if she takes a hard line she will be a bad parent who doesn't understand her kids' needs, but if she takes a softer approach she feels weak and ineffectual.

As a child, Maria didn't have many temper outbursts so finds her children's self-expression hard to handle. Her father was a very angry man and she was often fearful of his temper; it wasn't that he was violent, but his yelling and screaming always made her scared and uncomfortable. She tended to react as a child by suppressing her anger, partly because she didn't want to be like her father and partly out of fear of 'setting dad off'. Her mother tended to take a placating role and try to soothe her father's tantrums by giving him whatever he wanted.

Maria realizes that she doesn't know how to express anger properly and that her own children don't have an appropriate role model to learn from. She cannot show her kids how to have healthy anger when she doesn't know how herself. She also realizes that she has grown up thinking anger is bad and to be avoided at all costs, which is why her children's anger makes her feel so bad.

TOP TIPS FOR DEALING WITH YOUR ANGRY TEENAGER

In addition to employing all the techniques outlined in the rest of this book, here are some extra tips to help you cope:

1 Don't take it personally
It is hard not to when your teen is yelling that they hate you, but the reason that your children get so abusive with you is that they feel safe and secure with you. Their anger towards you is a compliment!

2 Don't retaliate
Remember that they are the child and you are the adult. Use all the techniques outlined so far and, if all else fails, take time out and calm down.

3 Think of your relationship
Consider your long-term relationship with your child, not the thing they did today that annoyed you. The long term is more important than a tidy room or a slammed door (isn't it?).

4 Tell your child how you feel
Be honest. Explain how their behaviour makes you feel hurt and angry. Children are notoriously self-centred (egocentric in psychology terms) and simply don't consider that you have feelings too.

5 Don't criticize

Try not to, in your anger, criticize your child – try to restrict your attack on their behaviour only, or you risk damaging their self-esteem through frequent character assassinations.

6 Be the role model

Let them learn how you manage and control your own anger (using the techniques in this book) – this is the best way for them to learn.

7 Reduce stressful moments

Anger is more likely to flare up at times of stress, so try to identify and reduce stressful triggers (such as when trying to get everyone off to school on time). Find ways to introduce more calm, by getting up earlier for example, so that meltdowns are less frequent – and to ensure that if they do happen, you are in a calmer state of mind to handle them.

Quick fix

Knowing that angry children are normal should help you to not take things too personally – which in turn can ensure that you don't get too angry in response yourself.

Having said all this, boundaries and discipline are vital to managing anger and hostility in your children. This means that they must accept that certain behaviours are no-goes. These include physical abuse (hitting or kicking you or other people), acts of aggression toward possessions (yours or theirs) and verbal abuse such as swearing. There should be clear and consistent consequences of breaking these rules, such as grounding, loss of privileges or pocket money, etc. If your kids do seem to be very aggressive or constantly and excessively hostile, it might be worth seeking professional guidance.

MOVING ON

While the material in the rest of this book will also be invaluable to parents of angry children (i.e. all parents!), this chapter has focused on the specific ways we can help our children, from toddlers to teens, develop anger management skills. At the same time it has offered you, as parents, help to handle your own reactions and cope with the meltdowns. The next chapter deals with specific rage-inducing situations that are common in today's fast-paced world.

Key points

1 It is normal for children to get angry and to express this anger in socially unacceptable ways such as crying, screaming and whining.

2 It is up to us as parents to try to teach our children more socially acceptable ways of dealing with their anger.

3 Children (and their parents) should accept that anger is not a bad thing to experience – it is how this anger is expressed and what is done with it that matters.

4 A lot of anger management for children is best carried out while the child is calm so as to help them cope when they do get angry.

5 Parents are the best role models for teaching their children effective anger management techniques.

10

Phone rage, air rage,
road rage...

How do you feel?
Answer 'true' or 'false' to the following statements.

- *Ringing call centres is likely to make me angry.*   T/F
- *Other people using mobile phones in public places often makes me angry.*   T/F
- *There is something about flying that often makes me angry.*   T/F
- *I often lose my cool in the supermarket.*   T/F
- *I often shout at other drivers.*   T/F
- *I often get angry with my computer.*   T/F

The more 'true' answers you gave the more likely it is that you are liable to various types of 'rage', from phone rage to road rage to air rage. Using real-life case studies, this chapter will show the serious consequences that can result from letting irritations get on top of us, and the reasons why certain situations are so rage inducing. Each section will also include tips on reducing susceptibility to that particular rage.

Phone rage

According to research reported by the British Association of Anger Management, we are much more likely to lose our temper when speaking on the phone than speaking to someone face to face. More than half the people questioned admitted to losing their temper over the phone 'in the past year' alone. The problem is so widespread that in 2008 the UK's Channel 4 even produced a documentary on the subject, aptly entitled 'Phone rage'.

What is it about talking on the phone that induces such rage? While part of the issue is to do with the medium (lack of facial cues, anonymity of caller, etc.), most phone rage seems to arise when we are speaking to businesses that provide a service – or are meant to. Such businesses have plenty of procedures in place that seem deliberately calculated to make customers angry. For a start, most large organizations these days use call centres and automated handling systems, both of which are known to be very frustrating for customers.

According to a BBC report (24 October 2002), the things most likely to anger call centre customers were annoying music, synthetic voices and endless menu options. The report was based on research by market analyst Mintel, which also found that 90 per cent of people felt that their experience of call centres left them feeling angry and frustrated.

According to the research, the most common complaint was being kept on hold, with the music being played while on hold annoying more than half of respondents. Automated phone systems were another source of irritation, with the most frustrating element being the lack of an option to pick that matched what the caller needed. In addition, almost a third of callers said they became frustrated when their call was routed through a seemingly endless menu of options.

Food for thought

A range of other factors can contribute to phone rage. Which of the following make you angry? Use a scale of 1 to 5, with 1 being most likely to make you angry and 5 being least likely to make you angry.

Factor	1	2	3	4	5
Encountering scripted responses or unnecessary use of jargon					
Being held in a queue (while being told how important your call is)					
Having to wait ages for your call to be answered					

Factor	1	2	3	4	5
Not understanding the call operator (or them not understanding you; many call centres are now located outside the UK)					
Not being able to speak to a real person					

How to interpret your score
The lower your score (and especially less than 10), the more likely you are to experience phone rage!

According to phonerage.org (a website for phone ragers), the factors that drive customers towards phone rage also include bad customer service, irritating telephone voice menu systems and junk phone calls. All these factors have one main trigger in common: frustration at having a goal blocked (the goal of accessing the help required). However, phone rage is unlikely to increase your chance of getting the input you need, as many call centre staff are advised not to accept abuse and may hang up on you.

Cope with your phone rage, then, by:

▶ anticipating difficulties; this means, for example, allowing plenty of time to make your call

▶ having something else to do in case of having to wait; check your emails or even read a book!

▶ asking for the name of the operator; even a first name will allow you to feel that they are a bit less anonymous

▶ having realistic expectations about what you want from the organization (see chapter 8)

▶ using the anger management techniques in the rest of this book to simmer down if you feel the red mist descend.

Quick fix
Always make sure that you have something else to do so as not to waste time while you are waiting for your call to be dealt with.

Phone rage can be a problem when it is you getting angry but it can be equally difficult to handle when you are the victim of someone else's phone rage (e.g. if you work in a call centre). According to the Healthy Working Lives website, a number of factors can increase the likelihood of a customer 'raging' at you if you are a call operator:

▶ The presence of a compensation culture
If customers who complain loudly enough perceive that getting angry will get them results, they will.

▶ Understaffing
Obviously, if you are understaffed, there is more work and less time to do it. This means the customer having to wait longer.

▶ Personal circumstances of callers
Some customers will have a lot of anger, resentment or self-esteem issues already. Some may have mental health problems.

▶ Unrealistic expectations
Clients may have unrealistically high expectations of what the organization can offer and just expect too much. Others may be seeking quick and easy solutions to long-term and complex problems.

Point to remember

The call operator is human too and often whatever is making you angry is not their fault. Try not to take your rage out on them.

If you are on the receiving end of phone rage, here are some specific tips on how to cope with angry callers (for general information on how to cope with angry customers, refer back to chapter 8).

1 Work out the reason for their anger – it might not be caused by the reason for their call (a faulty product) but by the process of the call (e.g. being passed from pillar to post).
2 Acknowledge the emotion (e.g. 'I understand that you must be feeling pretty frustrated by now.')
3 Empathize with the caller (e.g. 'Gosh, that sounds awful – you must be totally fed up with it all.')

4 Apologize if appropriate to do so (e.g. 'I'm really sorry you have been kept waiting for so long.')

5 Explain clearly how you can solve the problem (or why you can't).

Try to keep logs of any 'phone rage' incidents, using the following template. This can be fed back to your line manager so that they can try to take action where possible to protect you (e.g. improve their communication of expectations to customers).

Phone rage template

Reason for call	Trigger for phone rage	How caller expressed their anger	What changes organization could make

Mobile rage

This is a slightly different category of phone rage and involves either anger directed at our badly performing mobiles (cell phones) or anger directed at how other people are using their mobile phones in public spaces.

A poll conducted in 2011 for the US company Tealeaf by Harris Interactive showed that when our mobiles don't perform well (e.g. load slowly, have a poor connection), 38 per cent of users exhibit 'mobile rage', which includes cursing their phone (23 per cent), screaming at it (11 per cent) and even throwing it (4 per cent). The same survey showed that people get angrier about mobile phone problems than they do about getting stuck in traffic!

Myth buster
It isn't the loudness of other people's mobile phone conversations that annoys us so much, but the fact that we can only hear one side of the dialogue. And if that doesn't annoy people, there is always the problem of irritating ring tones.

Phone rage attack on bus

According to a report in *The Star* (24 April 2012), a teenager was left with a broken jaw after a phone rage incident on a bus in Doncaster. The youngster had been talking to a friend on his mobile phone when a couple on the bus asked him to be quiet. He continued his conversation at which point the couple attacked him by kneeing him in his face with such force that his jaw was broken in three places.

According to a team of British psychologists (Monk, Fellas and Ley, 2004), it is not just the irritation of loud voices talking about people we've never heard of or and don't care about that causes us to lose our cool. It seems that we also feel an innate need to listen when we can only hear one side of a conversation, the researchers say. Even if it's no louder than an ordinary two-way exchange, the fact that we can only hear half the conversation means that we instinctively attempt to listen in, almost as if we're expecting to join in. It is this 'need to listen' effect that they say can contribute to our anger levels.

Air rage

'UK airlines reported 1,486 significant or serious acts of air rage in a year, a 59 per cent increase over the previous year.'

Sunday Times report, July 2006

Air rage seems to be one of the fastest growing rages and it is fairly easy to see why. There are many reasons why the whole experience of flying is stressful for many people:

▶ Crowded conditions: Crowds, both in-flight and pre-flight (in the airport), can impinge on our need for personal space and make us feel stressed.
▶ Delays: Delays are common and frequent and can raise stress levels by adding both to our frustration at missing out on holiday time, for example, and to the time that we have to spend in crowded and increasingly unpleasant conditions. These stressors

can be exacerbated by lack of communication or information about the delay, which can lead to a feeling of lack of control – a significant stressor in itself.

▶ Intrusive security: With security becoming ever-more intensive and intrusive, security checks add to stress levels by encroaching further into our personal space and by increasing crowded conditions as we are herded through. Being asked personal questions can be irritating too, and not being allowed to carry certain things on to the plane, like water, can feel like an infringement of our rights (especially if we are forced to bin the forbidden items).

▶ Stress over baggage: Most airlines have weight and size restrictions on hand and other baggage and uncertainty about whether your luggage will meet the requirements can be stressful unless you are well prepared.

▶ Uncomfortable environment: Airports and planes can feel uncomfortably hot due to both overcrowding and wearing too many layers (perhaps to avoid carrying them in our weighed hand luggage).

▶ Smoking bans and drunkenness: These can add to the stress for smokers, while excessive alcohol consumption can lead to lowered inhibitions – making passengers more likely to erupt when things don't go right. According to a BBC report in 2001, 43 per cent of air rage incidents involved alcohol while 33 per cent revolved around the desire to smoke.

▶ High expectations: For many, their holiday starts when they close their front door, so when things get uncomfortable or stressful at the airport, there is the added disappointment that the much-anticipated holiday is off to such a poor start.

▶ Restricted resources: Lack of space and limited access to toilets, food and entertainment can all add to the stress, especially for families travelling with children. The strain of children competing with each other for resources ('It's my turn to play on the DS', 'It's my turn to sit next to Mummy', etc.) can strain even the most relaxed parent's patience.

All this can lead to a build-up of stress and anger that can erupt as 'air rage' or 'plane rage'. According to the BBC current affairs programme *4 × 4* (2001), nine out of ten cabin crew felt that air rage was actually putting lives at risk.

CASE STUDY

Air-rage fight over reclining seat forces United Airlines flight to return home

A report in *The Guardian* (1 June 2011) stated that F-16 fighter jets were needed to escort a Ghana-bound US plane back to Dulles airport after a fight broke out between two passengers on board.

Apparently tempers boiled over when one man reclined his seat into the lap of the man behind him. The conflict escalated and a fight broke out, during which a flight attendant and another passenger tried to intervene.

HOW TO AVOID AIR RAGE

Minimize your likelihood of letting your anger boil over in the following ways:

▶ Dress in layers than can be removed or added as required.
▶ Leave space in your hand luggage for removed items of clothing and for duty-free purchases so that you are not hauling several bags around the airport (and worrying about losing things).
▶ Check well in advance that your baggage meets the requirements and that you have no forbidden items; see the airline's website for their rules.
▶ Plan ahead if you travel with children to ensure that they have as much to occupy them as possible to limit squabbling.

Quick fix
The best way to minimize your likelihood of experiencing air rage is to follow the three 'Ps': plan, prepare and plot!

▶ Lower your expectations; expect stress and less than comfortable conditions rather than expecting things to be perfect. Your holiday should start when you land, not when you close your front door.
▶ Restrict alcohol intake and use nicotine patches if required.
▶ Use the crowded conditions to your advantage: strike up friendly conversations with your fellow 'inmates', network, find

like-minded people, etc. Rallying forces if there is a problem worth complaining about is always more effective than individual complaints. You might even also find a useful work contact!

When you next plan to fly, spend some time working through and visualizing your journey from start to finish, in order to identify 'air rage hotspots' or air rage triggers. Make a table like the one below to list your ideas (while you are calm) for how you might avoid or cope with the triggers.

Air rage hotspot	Trigger	Coping response
Leaving the house in the taxi	Spouse and children not ready	Tell them to be ready 15 minutes in advance, or order taxi earlier than needed.
Queues at airport check-in	Hot, noisy, crowded; children bored, nowhere to sit	Chat to neighbours in queue, bring iPod, DS or other entertainment for children, bring something useful for yourself (e.g. notebook).

Shopping rage

'Trolley rage' at supermarket

According to a BBC report (19 May 2003), a woman was attacked in a 'trolley rage' incident that left her bruised in an Ipswich supermarket. The incident happened when a shopper accidentally bumped another with her trolley. She apologized, but the other woman became verbally abusive and threatening, and then grabbed her arm tightly enough to cause bruising.

According to a report in the *Norwich Evening News* (25 May 2011), a shopper grew so angry with a member of staff at a supermarket that she rammed her trolley into her before throwing the trolley contents against a wall.

A court heard that the incident erupted over a dispute about payment for the shopper's groceries. The items she was buying had been scanned by the checkout operator but her payment card had to be re-entered because of some problem. The shopper became angry because she felt that re-entry of her card was unnecessary. The situation escalated until the shopper swore and rammed the trolley into the staff member's stomach.

Shopping or trolley rage is symptomatic of the Facebook generation, which wants everything and wants it now – and probably has little patience for shoppers who take a little longer over their shop. However, shopping rage is not caused only by impatience but by a host of other triggers:

- ▶ General raised stress levels mean that we are more prone to 'rage' (see chapter 3).
- ▶ The supermarket shop is not, for most people, a leisure activity; rather it is something that has to be squeezed into an otherwise hectic life, so time pressures add to the background of general stress.
- ▶ As in so many areas, our 'shoppers' rights' alert us to when our high expectations are not met, leading us to be angry when excellent customer service is not achieved (e.g. wrong prices, queues, checkout failure).
- ▶ Add to this mixture the unintentional (or intentional) rudeness of other shoppers as they inadvertently bump trolleys, abandon their trolley in the queue while they go back for a forgotten item, steal a parking space or commit another such real or imagined crime, and we have a potent mix ready to explode.

TROLLEY RAGE

According to a report in *The Daily Record* of 22 April 2011, half the population of Britain has suffered from trolley rage, while a fifth have stormed out of a shop after queuing for less than three minutes. A third admitted raising their voice or getting angry with shop staff and 20 per cent argued with other shoppers.

What are your triggers for trolley rage?

Which of the following triggers make you angry? Use a scale of 1 to 5, with 1 being most likely to make you angry and 5 being least likely to make you angry.

Trigger	1	2	3	4	5
Items being out of stock					
Children running in the aisles					
Cramped aisles					
Faulty trolleys					
Other shoppers bumping into me					
Rude staff					
Tills not taking off discounted prices					
Items priced wrongly					
Items going through tills at wrong price					
Self-service tills repeatedly alerting us to 'unexpected item in bagging area'					

CHANGING-ROOM RAGE

Related to trolley rage are other shopping rages, such as 'changing-room rage'. According to *The Daily Record* (22 April 2011), the UK 'has officially lost its temper' with 'changing-room rage' now joining the growing list of reasons to lose our cool. It seems that research has shown that almost 75 per cent of women have experienced changing-room rage while out shopping for clothes.

According to research conducted by retailers isme.com, symptoms of changing-room rage include snapping at retail assistants, losing our temper, abandoning clothes and leaving a store in fury. It seems that three-quarters of women are so angry with cramped, cluttered and poorly designed fitting rooms that they don't even bother trying on clothes. And six out of ten women admit to angrily leaving garments on the nearest rail rather than face a changing cubicle.

Whatever the type of shopping rage, the triggers are probably the same and to do with overall stress levels and 'hurry sickness'. The routes to managing them, then, are tied in around general stress-reducing and anger management measures, as outlined in chapters 5 and 6.

Quick fix
Lowering your general stress levels will reduce your likelihood of succumbing to trolley rage.

Road rage

> *'[Road rage is] an incident in which an angry or impatient motorist or passenger intentionally injures or kills another motorist, passenger, or pedestrian, or attempts or threatens to injure or kill another motorist, passenger, or pedestrian.'*
>
> Controlling Road Rage, pilot study, 1999

A survey carried out by the UK motoring organization Green Flag in 2007 found that eight out of ten drivers experienced some sort of road rage once a week or more. A US study carried out by the AAA found that at least 300 road rage incidents lead to injuries or fatalities every year.

In 2006 *The Sunday Times* reported that more than 80 per cent of drivers said they have been involved in road rage incidents; 25 per cent had committed an act of road rage themselves.

Road rage can include the following behaviours:

▶ Aggressive driving such as sudden acceleration or braking, or close tailgating (with the intention of putting pressure on the other car)
▶ Deliberately preventing someone from overtaking them or merging into their lane
▶ Trying to follow or chase other motorists who they feel have wronged them
▶ Flashing lights and/or sounding the horn excessively
▶ Making rude gestures
▶ Shouting verbal abuses or threats
▶ Getting out of the car in an attempt to confront another motorist
▶ Throwing objects from a car at another vehicle or other attempt to inflict damage.

Are you a potential road rager?

How much do the following statements apply to you?

Statement	1 Strongly disagree	2	3	4	5 Strongly agree
I drive as fast as I can get away with.					
I am always in a hurry when I drive.					
I am constantly switching lanes to try to save a few seconds' travelling time.					

(contd)

Statement	1 Strongly disagree	2	3	4	5 Strongly agree
It really bothers me when someone tries to cut in front of me.					
If another motorist does something I don't like, I make sure they know about it.					
I won't let another driver get away with cutting in front of me.					
I will drive very close behind a driver who has wronged me to make my point.					
I will often make a rude gesture to a driver who has wronged me.					
I will often shout abuse to a driver who has wronged me.					
Half the other drivers on the road are incompetent and don't know how to drive properly.					

How to interpret your score

Scores above 20 indicate an increased propensity to road rage. In other words, your attitude towards driving is such that you are more likely to be susceptible to road rage. You drive quickly and aggressively, may not leave yourself enough time to get to your destination on time and have a low tolerance for other people's mistakes. See chapter 3 in order to learn how to lower your stress levels and decrease your risk of succumbing to road rage.

Dublin man jailed for road rage killing

A BBC news report (23 April 2012) stated that a Dublin man was jailed for 12 years for killing a motorist in a road rage incident. The man pleaded guilty to the manslaughter and the court was told how the victim was hit on the head with a hurling stick, which caused the fatal injury.

The judge said it was the second road rage homicide to have appeared before him in a short space of time.

Police appeal after Ilkeston road rage attack

A BBC news report (21 April 2012) quoted a Derbyshire woman, who was knocked to the ground by a man in a road rage incident, as saying that she 'could have died' in the attack. The incident happened after the victim overtook him.

HOW TO COPE WITH SOMEONE'S ROAD RAGE

The chances are that your road rager is a stranger to you and that you are unlikely ever to see them again – unless you see them in court. Their attack on you is thus not likely to be personal; they are just poor at anger management. While it might be tempting to suggest to them that they read this book, they are not likely to take kindly to any well-intentioned advice on your part on how to learn to control their anger.

You can't therefore change their behaviour, but you can take control of your own. You can choose not to fight fire with fire and respond in a calm and controlled way (well, one of you has to). Try to follow the techniques outlined in chapter 7.

MANAGING YOUR OWN ROAD RAGE

If it is you on the verge of road rage, use the following tips to help stay cool.

▶ Develop empathy
Try to see the other driver's viewpoint, or imagine that they are related to you. The car that has just 'cut you up' may well be driven by an idiot who doesn't know how to drive, but they might be distracted or preoccupied with more serious matters: rushing to see a dying parent

in hospital or worried about a recent medical diagnosis. We never really know what is going on in other people's lives.

► If you can, apologize
Even if the incident is not strictly your fault, apologizing relieves tension for everyone and allows you to do the right thing (even if the other person doesn't).

► Keep perspective
You won't ever see the other person again so how much does the incident really matter? Try to 'perspectivize' by putting it into the grand scheme of things.

Point to remember

The other motorist may have troubles of their own which are causing them to drive inconsiderately. Bearing this in mind can help you empathize and stay cool.

Computer rage

'...71 per cent of internet users admit to having suffered net rage; 50 per cent of us have reacted to computer problems by hitting our PC, hurling parts of it around, screaming or abusing our colleagues.'

Sunday Times magazine, 16 July 2006

According to a 2009 report in the *Daily Telegraph*, more than half of Britons suffer from 'computer rage', which leads them verbally or even physically to attack their computers. Users become so frustrated with their computer equipment that they shout and swear at display screens, hit keyboards and smash mice to vent their anger. Most of us can relate to this – it is extremely frustrating, when we are trying to get something done, to be thwarted by technological failure (see chapter 1).

However, there are other reasons why so many of us tend to blow a fuse over computer failures. With more and more reliance in today's modern age on unpredictable technology, we are feeling more and more out of control. Most of us don't know how computers work and this lack of ability to understand what makes these machines

208

'tick' can lead to feelings of helplessness. We don't know how to fix them and rely on others to help us – and that help might be a long time coming. All this adds to our frustration until it explodes into rage. Even if we manage to control ourselves, we may only suppress our rage until we leave work, meaning that our ensuing road or trolley rage might, in fact, be stored-up computer rage.

HOW TO BEAT COMPUTER RAGE

The main reason for computer rage is that the technological problem creates delays in getting things done. A few simple measures can reduce the impact of computer failures, which, at some point, are inevitable.

▶ Always back up all your files
Store files online or transfer all necessary data to CDs and DVDs. In the event of a system crash, you can then always retrieve your files and work offline or on another machine while your own computer is being fixed.

▶ Stay calm
If you encounter an unexpected system error, don't hit your PC or thump your mouse. Instead, report the problem, then get up and walk away. Take a stroll, have a chat with your co-workers and friends or do another piece of work.

▶ Learn to troubleshoot
If you face the same problem regularly, get to know troubleshooting techniques. Learn from the techies who come to help you or try to attend training. If you turn a negative experience into a positive one you will be less stressed about the next problem.

▶ Work well ahead
Get into the habit of working well ahead for deadlines where possible. This means assuming that computers will crash and allowing time for this; then you will be pleasantly surprised if all goes smoothly and you are able to get ahead.

Point to remember

Computers do crash! They don't do it to annoy you personally, so avoid computer rage by not taking problems personally and being prepared for them to happen.

MOVING ON

This final chapter has dealt with some specific situations where you are likely to get into a rage, but the same broad rules for managing anger apply in these as in other circumstances. If you stop and think before reacting and look at the bigger picture, this will help you to put even the strongest rage trigger into perspective. By keeping calm and remembering not to take a problem personally, you will find that you can control your rage rather than have it control you.

Key points

1 A number of common trigger situations are likely to lead to rage.

2 Identifying and being aware of these 'hotspots' reduces your risk of losing it.

3 Lowering your overall stress levels reduces your chances of experiencing a 'rage'.

4 Anticipation and preparation are the keys to avoiding a lot of angry situations.

5 Common rages such as computer rage and trolley rage happen because things don't always go smoothly. Taking things personally fuels the rage, so it can help to remember that these happen to everyone.

References

Chapter 1

Mental Health Foundation: *Boiling Point: Problem anger and what we can do about it*, 2008. For the full report, go to: http://www.angermanage.co.uk

Dahlen, E.R. and Deffenbacher, J.L., 'Anger management' in Lyddon, J. W. (eds) *Empirically supported cognitive therapies: Current and future applications* (New York: Springer, 2001)

Sell, A., 'Formidability and the logic of human anger', in Tooby, J. and Cosmides, L., *Proceedings of the National Academy of Sciences*, August 2009

Chapter 2

Harburg, E., Erfurt, J.C., Hauenstein, L.S., et al., 'Socio-ecological stress, suppressed hostility, skin color, and black–white male blood pressure', *Psychosomatic Medicine*, 35, 276–96 (1973)

Harburg, E., Blakelock, E.H., and Roeper, P.J., 'Resentful and reflective coping with arbitrary authority and blood pressure', *Psychosomatic Medicine*, 41, 189–202 (1979)

Gentry, W.D., Chesney, A.P., Gary, H.E., et al., 'Habitual anger-coping styles. I. Effect on mean blood pressure and risk for essential hypertension', *Psychosomatic Medicine*, 44, 195–202 (1982)

Pernini, C., Muller, F.B., and Buhler, F.R., 'Suppressed aggression and hyperdynamic cardiovascular regulation in normotensive offspring of essential hypertensive patients', *J. Cardiovasc. Pharmacol.*, 12 (suppl 3): S130-S133 (1988)

Schneider, R.H., Egan, B.M., Johnson, E.H., Drobny, H., and Julius, S., 'Anger and anxiety in borderline hypertension' *Psychosomatic Medicine*, 48, 242–8 (1986)

Robins, S., and Novaco, R.W., 'Anger control as a health promotion mechanism', in Mostofsky, D., and Barlow, D. (eds), *The Management of Stress and Anxiety in Medical Disorders* (Boston: Allyn & Bacon, 2000)

Lineweber, C., Westerlund, H., Theorell, T., Kivimaki, M., Westerholm, P., and Alfredson, L. 'Covert coping with unfair treatment at work and risk of myocardial infacrction and cardiac death among men: prospective cohort study', *Journal of Epidemiology Community Health*, 0, 1–6 (2009)

Deffenbacher, J.L., Oetting, E.R., Lynch, R.A. and Morris, C.D., 'The expression of anger and its consequences', *Behaviour Research Therapy*, 34 (7) 575–90 (1996)

Fitness, J., 'Anger in the workplace: an emotional script approach to anger episodes between workers and their superiors, co-workers and subordinates', *Journal of Organizational Behaviour*, 21, 147–62 (2000)

Averill, J.R., *Anger and aggression: an essay on emotion* (New York: Springer-Verlag, 1982)

Thomas, S., Smucker, C., and Droppleman, P., 'It hurts most around the heart: a phenomological exploration of women's anger', *Journal of Advanced Nursing*, 28 (2), 311–22 (1998)

Miron-Spektor, E., and Rafaeli, A., 'The effects of anger in the workplace: when, where and why observing anger enhances or hinders performance', *Research in Personnel and Human Resources Management* (Bradford: Emerald Group Publishing, 2009)

Booth, J., 'An investigation into the causes, characteristics and consequences of anger in the workplace' (unpublished thesis submitted to the University of Central Lancashire, 2010)

Chapter 3

Mental Health Foundation: *Boiling Point: Problem anger and what we can do about it*, 2008. For the full report, go to: http://www.angermanage.co.uk

Forgays, D.G., Forgays, D.K., and Spielberger, C. D., 'Factor structure of the state-trait anger expression inventory', *Journal of Personality Assessment,* 69(3), 497–507 (1997)

Martin, R., Watson, D., and Wan, C.K., 'A three-factor model of trait anger: Dimensions of affect, behavior, and cognition', *Journal of Personality,* 68(5), 869–97 (2000)

Chapter 4

Mental Health Foundation: *Boiling Point: Problem anger and what we can do about it,* 2008. For the full report, go to: http://www. angermanage.co.uk

Chapter 5

Fletcher, Damien, 'What makes the British such angry people and how to keep your cool', http://www.mirror.co.uk/news/top-stories/2009/05/15/

http://www.dailymail.co.uk/femail/article-1380989/ 28 April 2011

Baron, R.A., *Human aggression* (New York: Plenum Press, 1977).

Stosny, Steven, *Treating attachment abuse: a compassionate approach* (New York: Springer, 1995)

Norris, R., Carroll, D., and Cochrane, R., 'The effects of physical activity and exercise training on psychological stress and wellbeing in an adolescent population', *J Psychosom Res.,* 36:55–65 (1992)

Stewart, K.J., Turner, K.L., Bacher, A.C., DeRegis, J.R., Sung, J., Tayback, M., and Ouyang, P., 'Are fitness, activity, and fatness associated with health-related quality of life and mood in older persons?' *J Cardiopulm Rehabil.,* 23: 115–21 (2003)

Tkacz, J., Young-Hyman, D., Boyle, C.A., and Davis, C.L., 'Aerobic Exercise Program Reduces Anger Expression Among Overweight Children', *Pediatr Exerc Sci.* 20(4): 390–401 (November 2008)

Dutton, D.C., and Aron, A.P., 'Some evidence for heightened sexual attraction under conditions of high anxiety', *Journal of Personality and Social Psychology,* 30, 10–17 (1974)

Chapter 6

McKay, M., and Rogers, P., *The anger control workbook* (Oakland: New Harbinger Publications, 2000)

Moran, C., and Massam, M., 'An evaluation of humour in emergency work', *The Australasian Journal of Disaster and Trauma Studies* (1997)

Perls, F., Hefferline, R.F., and Goodman, P., *Gestalt therapy* (Oxford: Dell, 1965)

Chapter 7

Thomas, K. and Kilmann, R., *Thomas-Kilmann Conflict Mode Instrument* (New York: Xicom, 1997)

Chapter 8

Sunday Times Magazine, 18 July 2006

Gibson, D.E., and Barsade, S.G., 'The Experience of Anger at Work: Lessons from the Chronically Angry', presented at the Academy of Management, Chicago, Illinois (1999)

Mann, S., *Hiding What We Feel, Faking What We Don't* (London: Vega, 1999)

Chapter 9

Green, J.A., and Whitney, P.G., 'Screaming, yelling, whining and crying: categorical and intensity differences in vocal expressions of anger and sadness in children's tantrums', *Emotion,* Vol 11, no. 5, 1124–33 (2011)

Goodenough, F.L., *Anger in Young Children* (Minneapolis: University of Minnesota Press, 1931)

Potegal, M., and Davidson, R.J., 'Temper tantrums in young children', *Developmental and Behavioural Pediatrics* 24, 148–54 (2003)

Tavis, C., *Anger: the Misunderstood Emotion* (New York: Simon and Schuster, 1989)

Chapter 10

http://www.phonerage.org/

http://www.tealeaf.com/news/news-releases/2011/Tealeaf-Announces-New-Mobile-Research.php

Monk, A., Fellas, E., and Ley, E., 'Hearing only one side of normal and mobile phone conversations', *Behaviour & Information Technology* Vol 23, Issue 5, 301–5, 2004

BBC news report on 4 × 4, 'Trouble in the Air', 23 July 2001

Rathbone, D.B., and Huckabee, J.C., 'Controlling Road Rage: A Literature Review and Pilot Study Prepared for the AAA Foundation for Traffic Safety' (MSCE, June 1999)

Green Flag 2007: http://www.smartdriving.co.uk

The British Association of Anger Management: http://www.angermanage.co.uk

Healthy Working Lives: http://www.healthyworkinglives.com

The Daily Record: dailyrecord.co.uk, 22 April 2011

The Daily Telegraph, Murray Wardrop, 1 April 2009

Index